This Journal Belongs to

PROGRESS,
NOT PERFECTION

A Goal Journal for
Embracing Your Journey

MARY FLANNERY

STERLING
New York

STERLING
New York

An Imprint of Sterling Publishing Co., Inc.

ISBN 978-1-4549-4472-0

Distributed in Canada by Sterling Publishing Co., Inc.
C/o Canadian Manda Group, 664 Annette Street
Toronto, Ontario, Canada M6S 2C8
Distributed in the United Kingdom by GMC Distribution Services
Castle Place, 166 High Street, Lewes, East Sussex, England BN7 1XU
Distributed in Australia by NewSouth Books
University of New South Wales, Sydney, NSW 2052, Australia

For information about custom editions, special sales,
and premium and corporate purchases, please contact
Sterling Special Sales at specialsales@sterlingpublishing.com

Manufactured in Malaysia

2 4 6 8 10 9 7 5 3 1

www.sterlingpublishing.com

Text by Mary Flannery
Design by Christine Heun
Cover design and illustration by Julia Morris

Picture Credits: Getty Images: aleksandarvelasevic/DigitalVision Vectors
(boxes, arrows); Mitoria/iStock/Getty Images Plus (swirls)

Your Year of Progress

Hello, and welcome to the journey! Kudos to you for deciding you have a goal that's so important to you that you're going to spend the next year working toward it. It's that commitment that will get you where you want to go. More than talent, more than genius, more than anything else, being committed to a goal and working on it every day is what *actually* makes dreams come true.

Writing about your journey as you go along is an extraordinarily effective tool for keeping up your dedication. When you commit yourself on paper, you're letting your brain know, *We're taking this seriously. This is going to happen!* That kind of positive thinking is what keeps you motivated, no matter what challenges you face. On these pages, you're going to make your goal specific, set an actionable plan for achieving it, and train your brain to embrace success as an inevitable fact instead of an if.

Of course, every journey has its twists and turns, and this journal will help you navigate them. You'll see how you can overcome self-doubt, the urge to procrastinate, and even the impulse to quit. You'll see that beating yourself up and pushing yourself past your limits isn't how you reach your goal. Self-love and self-care are how you get there. Knowing when to rest is how you get there. Letting go of obstructive ideas—like perfection and what other people think—and instead embracing your beautiful, true self are how you get there. You're going to explore all these ideas and more on this journey.

While the road is long and the work can be hard, know that there is joy and meaning in the endeavor. By the end of this journal, you'll likely find that the journey itself matters as much as the goal. Working toward something you value with your whole heart means you're living your purpose, doing something you love to do. While that's not always easy, it is deeply gratifying and worthwhile. In fact, it's why you keep going. Not just because your goal is transcendent, but because getting there is itself a transcendent act. The joy really is in the journey and in the person you become along the way.

WHO YOU ARE. People often say that if you want to be happy, "Just be your-self." That sounds easy, but knowing your gorgeous, ever-changing self is a lifelong practice. And knowing yourself is *crucial* to setting the right goal and making progress toward it. Self-knowledge allows you to set your sights on what will truly make you happy, instead of getting caught up striving for stuff you think you should want but don't actually care about. This week is all about getting to your core so you can set the right goal.

WRITE NOW! Think about yourself. Not your job or your hobbies or the role you play for others—mother, friend, etc., important as those might be—but the things that are true about you regardless of everything else.

This above all: to thine own self be true.

—William Shakespeare

WHAT'S IMPORTANT. Now that you've thought about who you are on a deep level, it's time to think about what's really important—deep-down—to you.

WRITE NOW! What are your top priorities? List some of the things you want for yourself, not just now but in the grand story of your life.

_____

_____

_____

_____

_____

PRIORITIZE. Not every goal or aspiration is created equal. Even though they are all important to you, some probably feel more urgent than others.

WRITE NOW! Rank your priorities from least important to most important.

_____

_____

_____

_____

_____

_____

DEEP DOWN. Your priorities all came from somewhere, and knowing their sources can help you see which ones are crucial to you down to your core and which ones might be superficial. This is a brutally honest part of the process, where you have to look at your priorities and weed out the ones that came to you from societal dictates or from comparing yourself to others, instead of looking within. Deep priorities that come from the core of you help you create goals that are actually worth your time and energy.

WRITE NOW! Where do your priorities come from? Don't pull any punches here; be as honest with yourself as you possibly can.

HOW DO YOU FEEL? It's time to drill down on your priorities and how they make you feel. Sometimes we can decide that something so super important to us but then realize it also feels like a burden. You're evaluating your priorities to help you set a big goal for the coming year, and it's essential for that goal to be affirming, rewarding, or exciting to you, instead of something that feels like a millstone around your neck.

WRITE NOW! How do you really feel about your top priorities? Which ones are you the most excited about? Do any of them stress you out more than excite you?

To know what you prefer, instead of humbly saying Amen to what the world tells you you ought to prefer, is to have kept your soul alive.

—Robert Louis Stevenson

COMING TOGETHER. After reflecting on yourself and your priorities for five days, a solid conception of your goal should be coming together in your mind—one that incorporates your core values and has you raring to go.

WRITE NOW! Have this week's reflections changed your mind or your thinking about what your goal might be?

➥

_____

_____

_____

_____

PROGRESS, NOT PERFECTION. Reflect on your journal entries from the past week. Do you feel like you've made progress? Do you feel like you've enjoyed the journey and showed yourself love and care, or did you get hung up on perfection? Fill in the following progress bars to show how you feel about the week.

	1	5	10
Progress			
Enjoyment of the Journey			
Feelings of Self-Love			

WRITE NOW! What are your thoughts about this past week? Where did you make progress, and how did it feel?

➥

_____

_____

DREAM BIG. It's time to blue-sky it! What if you knew, without a doubt, that whatever your goal was you'd achieve it? What if the sky wasn't even the limit? Try thinking of your goal as a wish you just have to work for. Don't let yourself be held back by doubts or fears or even reality. What would your goal look like if there were nothing to stop you from achieving it?

WRITE NOW! What is the most grandiose, out-of-this-world version of what you want to achieve over the coming year?

What goals would you be setting for yourself if you knew you could not fail?

—Robert H. Schuller

WHY NOT? Now that you've imagined your goal as big as it can be, is there anything standing in the way of your getting there?

WRITE NOW! What obstacles do you think are blocking the path to your big, glorious goal?

_____

_____

_____

_____

_____

HOW REAL ARE THEY? Do any of those obstacles violate the laws of physics, time, or space? If not, odds are you can overcome them if you just believe you can and put in the work.

WRITE NOW! Which of those obstacles can you overcome? How would you begin?

_____

_____

_____

_____

_____

GET IT DOWN. You've looked inside yourself and all around you to find a goal that matters and grow it as big as you can. It's time to put that big goal of yours on paper in great, glowing detail. Instead of thinking of your goal in broad terms, like "I want to get fit," think about what that fitness means to you in body, mind, and spirit. It's not just about changing a number on a scale or in a bank account, it's about what those numbers mean and why they're important to you.

WRITE NOW! What would attaining your goal mean to you in body, mind, and spirit?

MAKE IT REAL. Picturing yourself achieving your goal is a key step toward getting there. Imagining what it will be like having accomplished your goal a year from now in vivid detail will make your mind see the goal as a reality, and getting your brain fully onboard is one of the most powerful early steps you can take. Convincing yourself that your goal is not just a dream but your future reality is progress in itself, and the more detail you can imagine, the better this exercise works.

WRITE NOW! Describe yourself a year from now, goal well met. Include as many sensory details as you can to create a vibrant, living picture.

_____

_____

_____

_____

_____

_____

_____

_____

_____

_____

In order to get what you want,
you need to know what you want.

—Debra Eckerling

GOOD REASONS. If you're going to spend a year working toward your goal, it had better be worth it, right!? You'll have to have some really good, really big reasons to stick with it.

WRITE NOW! What are the pros and cons for sticking with your goal? The pros should hopefully outweigh the cons.

_____

_____

_____

_____

PROGRESS, NOT PERFECTION. Reflect on your journal entries from the past week. Do you feel like you've made progress? Do you feel like you've enjoyed the journey and showed yourself love and care, or did you get hung up on perfection? Fill in the following progress bars to show how you feel about the week.

	1	5	10
Progress			
Enjoyment of the Journey			
Feelings of Self-Love			

WRITE NOW! What are your thoughts about this past week? Where did you make progress, and how did it feel?

_____

_____

MAKE A PLAN. Just as it's important to have a clear and detailed vision of your goal, it's equally important to have a clear plan for getting there. *Work hard* is a key element, maybe even a mantra, but it is not a plan. A plan has steps that start where you are and bring you steadily toward where you want to be. Sometimes it's hard to see what those steps might be. If that's the case for you, imagine already having achieved your goal and working backward from that point. This can help you see all the steps that brought you there.

WRITE NOW! What is your overall plan for reaching your goal, outlined in broad steps?

People who most frequently reach their goals are those who write them down and develop a plan to reach them.

—Susan B. Wilson

THE HARD PARTS. There are probably some steps in your plan that you're feeling nervous about.

WRITE NOW! What parts of the plan stress you out or seem as if they will be really difficult to accomplish?

_____

_____

_____

_____

_____

PLANNING FOR YOUR PLAN. Since you've already identified the hard steps, now make a plan for dealing with them.

WRITE NOW! What can you do to help yourself get through those hard steps?

_____

_____

_____

_____

_____

_____

PHASING IN. Breaking up a plan into a series of phases can be exception-ally helpful. Phases not only give you a series of achievable goals that will feel good to meet, but they also help you determine what you need to do in greater detail. And as you've seen already, the more details you have, the easier progress becomes. Think about the steps of your plan and how you can break them out into phases of smaller goals. You can set them as calendar goals if you're deadline-oriented or, if you're more into finishing projects than hitting dates, set the goals as mini projects.

WRITE NOW! Write down each phase of your plan and the goals you want to hit for them.

DREAM ON. Just because you now have a set plan in place doesn't mean you can't keep dreaming. As you progress toward your goal over the coming year, that goal might change. It might grow even bigger, it might grow into something else, it might generate new goals you haven't even imagined yet. Staying flexible as you grow will take you to the place you're meant to be, which is better than aiming at the place you only thought you wanted to be.

WRITE NOW! Daydream about getting to your goal. What comes up that you haven't planned for yet? This can be a new hard-and-fast detail or something that's pure fun.

Without leaps of imagination, or dreaming,
we lose the excitement of possibilities.
Dreaming, after all, is a form of planning.

—Gloria Steinem

STEP ON IT. Setting your goal and making a plan for getting there is quite a lot of progress in itself. Now it's time to start actualizing those ideas and putting your plan into action!

WRITE NOW! What is the very first thing you're going to do to step toward your goal today?

_____

_____

_____

_____

PROGRESS, NOT PERFECTION. Reflect on your journal entries from the past week. Do you feel that you've made progress? Do you feel like you've enjoyed the journey and showed yourself love and care, or did you get hung up on perfection? Fill in the following progress bars to show how you feel about the week.

	1	5	10
Progress			
Enjoyment of the Journey			
Feelings of Self-Love			

WRITE NOW! What are your thoughts about this past week? Where did you make progress, and how did it feel?

_____

_____

PERFECT IMPEDIMENT. Nothing stops you from reaching a goal, or even making progress, like the idea of perfection. Envisioning a goal as unachieved until it's perfect is buying into an impossible myth, because perfection is a human-made concept that exists exactly nowhere in the real world. There are no perfect trees or perfect days, just trees and days and how you think about them. This is why you will never reach complete perfection, but you can find so much good in getting toward your perfectly imperfect goals.

WRITE NOW! How do you feel about the idea of perfection? How has it influenced your journey?

Striving for perfection is a demoralizing and guaranteed formula for failure. Striving for excellence, on the other hand, is motivating.

—Harriet Braiker

PERFECTLY IMPERFECT. Your quirks and imperfections are essential parts of what make you uniquely you and uniquely wonderful.

WRITE NOW! What are your favorite quirks and imperfections in yourself?

IMPERFECTLY PERFECT. There are also parts of you that you probably see as imperfect and want to change, but can't. Accepting and loving those parts is the greatest kindness you can do for yourself.

WRITE NOW! Write a love note to a part of you that you've been mean to or mad at in the past.

HANG UP THAT HANG-UP. It's easy to get hung up trying to do something perfectly. But trying to be perfect can make you miss or dismiss some really great accomplishments or, worse, it can prevent you from ever getting anywhere. Reaching for perfection, you might never feel like anything is ever finished or, if you do finish something, you can only see flaws in it. Boo on that! Perfection, like comparison, is the thief of joy. If you just hang up on it, you'll start to see the whole picture instead of just the cracks in the paint.

WRITE NOW! What are some accomplishments you've had that you've pooh-poohed because they weren't perfect? Sing their praises now!

WHAT A RELIEF! Giving up on perfection is an incredibly freeing thing to do. It lets light and love and laughter and all that good stuff into whatever you're doing. Instead of making a grueling trek toward an impossibility, you can make a joyful journey of self-discovery and improvement. And all it takes is just a shift in attitude. Instead of demanding perfection of yourself, all you need to do is make a little progress, do a little victory dance over it, and repeat. And if you backslide now and then, who cares? No one's perfect.

WRITE NOW! What have you been trying to do perfectly? How can you change your approach so, instead of striving toward an impossible ideal, you enjoy the process of getting "good"?

_____

_____

_____

_____

_____

_____

_____

_____

_____

*And now that you don't have
to be perfect, you can be good.*

—John Steinbeck

WABI-SABI. That's the Japanese term for loving the inevitable imperfections in life. The cracks in the glaze of a ceramic vase, a weirdly shaped tomato, that scar on your knee. There is beauty to be found in the imperfect.

WRITE NOW! What is your favorite imperfect thing about your journey so far?

_____

_____

_____

_____

_____

PROGRESS, NOT PERFECTION. Reflect on your journal entries from the past week. Do you feel like you've made progress? Do you feel like you've enjoyed the journey and showed yourself love and care, or did you get hung up on perfection? Fill in the following progress bars to show how you feel about the week.

	1	5	10
Progress			
Enjoyment of the Journey			
Feelings of Self-Love			

WRITE NOW! What are your thoughts about this past week? Where did you make progress, and how did it feel?

_____

_____

HOW'S IT GOING? You've been working on making progress on your plan for a week now and maybe you're experiencing highs and lows of feeling superpowered and entirely discouraged and then back again. Or maybe you're feeling increasingly determined with a fire under your butt to keep making progress. Or maybe you've had some other experience entirely. There is no right or wrong way—there is only your journey.

WRITE NOW! How are you feeling about your journey and your progress?

_____

_____

_____

_____

_____

_____

_____

_____

*After the novelty of chasing your big
dream has subsided, chances are you'll be
swallowed by a tsunami of self-doubt....
If you are feeling disheartened, take a breath.
Remember that self-doubt is normal.*

—Marie Forleo

GOING AT YOUR OWN PACE. Everyone makes progress at their own pace, whether slow and steady or filled with fits and starts.

WRITE NOW! What is your pace like?

_____

_____

_____

_____

_____

_____

SPIRIT ANIMAL. Find a mascot to cheer you on. Maybe you feel connected to the steady tortoise, the stop-and-go hare, or another animal entirely.

WRITE NOW! What animal is your pacing mascot? Do you feel like thinking of that particular animal as a mascot will help you?

_____

_____

_____

_____

_____

WHEN THE GOING GETS TOUGH. When you're still near the start of a journey, sometimes the long road ahead can feel overwhelming. The next big hill or high hurdle makes you want to turn around and just go home, back to where you were before you decided to do this thing. Knowing that these moments can and will happen helps take the edge off. If you plan for them, you can beat them, and one of the best weapons against feeling overwhelmed is visualizing your purpose. Remembering why you're on this journey in the first place and picturing where it will take you if you just stick to the road will keep you going.

WRITE NOW! Write yourself a pep talk, reminding yourself in vivid detail about your goal.

ONE STEP AT A TIME. It's easy to want to run ahead in a plan, to make a big leap of progress or to get to a step you think is going to be a really good one. But when you're on a long journey—*especially* when you're on a long journey—it's crucial to go one step at a time so you don't get ahead of yourself. If you try to do something too big from too far down the line before you're ready for it, you could set yourself up for disappointment. Each step on your journey is an important one that you can appreciate if you take the time to see its worth.

WRITE NOW! What is your greatest asset for making progress at this moment?

_____

_____

_____

_____

_____

_____

_____

_____

_____

Do what you can, with what you've got, where you are.

—Squire Bill Widener

REMEMBER TO REST. Rest is an important component of keeping your pace. You can't be all progress all the time.

WRITE NOW! What helps you relax and feel truly rested?

_____

_____

_____

_____

_____

PROGRESS, NOT PERFECTION. Reflect on your journal entries from the past week. Do you feel like you've made progress? Do you feel like you've enjoyed the journey and showed yourself love and care, or did you get hung up on perfection? Fill in the following progress bars to show how you feel about the week.

	1	5	10
Progress			
Enjoyment of the Journey			
Feelings of Self-Love			

WRITE NOW! What are your thoughts about this past week? Where did you make progress, and how did it feel?

_____

_____

THE TRUTH. When you're on a journey of self-improvement or moving toward a specific goal, it can feel like you're in the process of becoming something whole or complete. You might think that until you get to that finish line, you're coming up short, but the truth is that we are all always in process but we are also always whole and complete. Achieving perfection is a myth partly because you are already perfect. Being on the road somewhere and getting better at something doesn't diminish who you are now. Learning to fully love and appreciate yourself right now allows you to love and appreciate the journey and get to your goal with joy.

WRITE NOW! In what ways have you been feeling less than whole and complete? How can you prove yourself wrong?

_____

_____

_____

_____

_____

_____

_____

_____

The truth of my Being is that I was created perfect, whole, and complete.

—Louise Hay

LITTLE VICTORIES. Reaching small goals, including just the act of keeping track, are the little victories that keep us feeling good on our journey.

WRITE NOW! What little victory have you experienced lately?

➯
_____

_____

_____

_____

_____

_____

SAVOR. Each little win is a victory, and these victories can have an even greater impact if you take the time to reflect on and savor them.

WRITE NOW! What did your latest little victory feel like?

➯
_____

_____

_____

_____

_____

_____

ALL HAIL AFFIRMATIONS. These short, positive, powerful statements can be a big help in keeping you on track and motivated. If you repeat an affirmation every day, even if you don't totally believe it at first, it sinks into your mind and your brain starts to buy it. In this way, an affirmation can challenge and dispel negative thinking and bolster you on your journey. The keys to coming up with a powerful affirmation are making it present tense and positive (*I am reaching my goal,* not *I won't quit. I am powerful and capable,* instead of *I am getting stronger*). It should also resonate emotionally—you should feel something when you say it.

WRITE NOW! Try coming up with some affirmations of your own to keep you feeling strong and motivated or encouraged in any way you might need.

YOU ARE GOLDEN. There is a story about a golden Buddha statue at a monastery in Thailand that was covered in plaster and pieces of glass by monks so an invading army wouldn't plunder it. After a long time, everyone forgot that the statue wasn't made of plaster but then one day a monk meditating near it saw a chunk of plaster fall away and realized that the Buddha was really golden. In a way, we were all born golden, but then the world and our experiences pile expectations on us that make us think we're merely plaster.

WRITE NOW! What has been piled on you that might get in the way of your goal—of you realizing that you're golden?

Each of us is golden by nature. We were born golden . . . [but] we developed a casing of stone. . . . Then something comes along that cracks our casing.

—Alan Cohen

YES, YOU ARE. In many ways, this week was about realizing how good you already are. When you reflect your own awesomeness (yes, you are awesome!), you often discover something new about yourself. It might be something awesome you hadn't noticed before or even that you're not comfortable thinking about being awesome.

WRITE NOW! What did you discover about yourself this week?

_____

_____

_____

_____

PROGRESS, NOT PERFECTION. Reflect on your journal entries from the past week. Do you feel like you made progress? Do you feel like you enjoyed the journey and showed yourself love and care, or did you get hung up on perfection? Fill in the following progress bars to show how you feel about the week.

	1	5	10
Progress			
Enjoyment of the Journey			
Feelings of Self-Love			

WRITE NOW! What are your thoughts about this past week? Where did you make progress, and how did it feel?

_____

_____

DON'T HOLD YOURSELF BACK. Sometimes we limit the progress we make because we've decided we can't do something or overcome something. That belief—whether you've consciously acknowledged it yet or not—is the root cause of what's holding you back. The thing itself is figure-outable. It might be hard and take work and require big changes, but that doesn't make it impossible. The only thing that makes it impossible is thinking it's impossible.

WRITE NOW! What limiting beliefs do you have that are getting in your way?

What's holding you back is your thought that something is holding you back.

—Ralph Marston

WHERE DID YOU COME FROM? The *you* in this question is that limiting belief you uncovered yesterday. Part of getting rid of it is knowing where it came from.

WRITE NOW! So where did that belief come from anyway?

BREAKING UP IS HARD TO DO. Letting go of a belief that's long gotten in your way doesn't happen overnight. It's a process that starts with telling that belief that it's gotta go.

WRITE NOW! Break up with that limiting belief in a short farewell note.

SO WRONG. Another step toward getting rid of a belief that's held you back is taking it apart and examining what's wrong with it. There are bound to be some misapprehensions and probably some old wounds in there. Bringing them into the light of day isn't easy and it might even hurt a little. You'll have to pry your heart open to take an honest look at something that probably is bound up with fear and shame. But, in the end, being free of a false limitation can bring on renewed progress and joy.

WRITE NOW! What's wrong with your limiting beliefs? What is literally incorrect about them?

BIG STRETCH. Now that you *know* what's wrong with the beliefs that have held you back, it's time to *prove* they're wrong. To finally rid yourself of a bad belief once and for all requires you to dig deep to find the strength to do what you've believed to be impossible. You have to stretch outside your comfort zone by doing at least a small piece of the thing you thought you couldn't do. This kind of progress amounts to a monumental step on any journey and can help make your goal feel all the more real.

WRITE NOW! What will you do to prove that belief wrong? Make a mini plan for traveling outside your comfort zone.

_____

_____

_____

_____

_____

_____

_____

_____

It takes strength to push through whatever is holding you back. You build your strength, in part, by stretching yourself.

—Valorie Burton

CONGRATULATE YOURSELF. This week was a tough one! You took a hard look at what's been holding you back and took steps to overcome it. Time to pat yourself on the back!

WRITE NOW! Congratulate yourself for doing the hard work.

_____

_____

_____

_____

_____

PROGRESS, NOT PERFECTION. Reflect on your journal entries from the past week. Do you feel that you've made progress? Do you feel like you enjoyed the journey and showed yourself love and care, or did you get hung up on perfection? Fill in the following progress bars to show how you feel about the week.

	1	5	10
Progress			
Enjoyment of the Journey			
Feelings of Self-Love			

WRITE NOW! What are your thoughts about this past week? Where did you make progress, and how did it feel?

_____

_____

YOU LOVE YOU. The whole reason you're on this journey is because you love you. It's true! If you didn't love yourself at all, you wouldn't care enough to try to do something like this in the first place. And if you're comfortable in your self-love, you already know that you're doing this for you. You know that the very act of trying to reach a goal, to make progress at all, is an act of self-love.

WRITE NOW! Have a self-love fest and write down all the things you love about yourself.

_____

_____

_____

_____

_____

_____

_____

_____

_____

Love yourself first and everything else falls into line. You really have to love yourself to get anything done in this world.

—attributed to Lucille Ball

STEP WITH CARE. As you saw, your journey started from love, whether you knew it or not, and it's important to bring that love with you every step of the way.

WRITE NOW! List a few ways you can treat yourself with a little more love and care on your journey.

_____

_____

_____

_____

_____

SUPPORT YOURSELF. One way to show yourself love is make sure you have the support you need.

WRITE NOW! Where do you need a little more support, and how can you get it?

_____

_____

_____

_____

_____

_____

THAT LOVING FEELING. Self-love is something many people struggle to embrace. It can feel awkward or egotistical or foreign to be loving and kind toward yourself, but it's something you can learn to do with more and more ease. And the more you love yourself, the harder you're going to work for you! To conjure up feelings of self-love, start by imagining the love you feel for a treasured friend or family member. That warmth, that joy, that ooey-gooey goodness. Really feel it. Now turn that feeling on yourself. Picture yourself embraced by that warm light of love.

WRITE NOW! How does it feel to actively bring up feelings of self-love?

BRING IT WITH YOU. If you can bring the spark of self-love with you on your journey—if you take each step with love and acceptance for yourself—no matter how things go and what you do or don't do, you'll win. That love will fuel your fire to keep progressing toward your goal, but it will also keep you warm when you hit a roadblock or change course or anything else. Because you'll always be you and if you love and accept yourself, you've already succeeded.

WRITE NOW! How does your self-love help and inspire you?

The greatest success is successful self-acceptance.

—Ben Sweet

MIRROR, MIRROR. A great way to tell yourself you love yourself is by literally telling yourself that you love *you*. Look in a mirror and tell yourself *I love you*. It might be awkward, but it's also powerful.

WRITE NOW! How did you feel during the mirror exercise?

_____

_____

_____

_____

_____

PROGRESS, NOT PERFECTION. Reflect on your journal entries from the past week. Do you feel like you made progress? Do you feel like you enjoyed the journey and showed yourself love and care, or did you get hung up on perfection? Fill in the following progress bars to show how you feel about the week.

	1	5	10
Progress			
Enjoyment of the Journey			
Feelings of Self-Love			

WRITE NOW! What are your thoughts about this past week? Where did you make progress, and how did it feel?

_____

_____

IT'S ALL FOR YOU. There is real joy in working toward a goal from a place of self-love, making progress for your own sake and no one else's. On the other hand, when you strive to be better than others, using them as the yardstick of your success, there will be a pebble in your shoe to trouble you on your journey. This is because you can always find someone you think is doing better than you, so you will always come up short, no matter how much progress you make. And joy gained from a sense of superiority will always have a sour note to it.

WRITE NOW! What is your yardstick of success?

There is nothing noble in being superior to some other [person]. The true nobility is in being superior to your previous self.

—W. L. Sheldon

YOUR OWN SUCCESS. Success looks different for everyone and for every goal. Its value to you is defined by you.

WRITE NOW! How do you define and value success?

FALSE DICHOTOMY. It can seem like there are only two options: success or failure. But there's an immense spectrum between the two and complete successes or failures are rare.

WRITE NOW! What would a total failure look like to you? Have you already progressed past that?

SO FAR, SO GOOD. At this point you've proven to yourself how committed you are to your goal. You've been working on it for a bunch of weeks, and you've probably experienced some ups and downs. No matter where you are in your plan and how you've felt about your progress, the fact that you're still on the journey is a massive accomplishment. You will get there if you just keep going. As you've probably realized by now, just showing up is half the battle. The work itself just rolls right along once you start.

WRITE NOW! What ups and downs have you experienced on this journey so far?

THE LITTLE THINGS. Success isn't always a ticker-tape parade with a marching band. Sometimes it's gaining one hard-fought inch on your journey, sometimes it's coming back after a setback, sometimes it's just showing up. Recognizing all your successes, even the quiet ones that others may not notice, is the fuel you need to keep going. It's also the joy that makes the journey so worthwhile.

WRITE NOW! What quiet successes have you had that perhaps other people don't see or you didn't even notice until you took a moment to reflect on them?

Success can be a quiet and hidden thing.

—Pam Brown

TREAT YOURSELF. Marking your progress with a little treat is a great way to show yourself some love and celebrate your successes.

WRITE NOW! What little treat will you give yourself or do for yourself to celebrate your journey so far?

PROGRESS, NOT PERFECTION. Reflect on your journal entries from the past week. Do you feel like you made progress? Do you feel like you enjoyed the journey and showed yourself love and care, or did you get hung up on perfection? Fill in the following progress bars to show how you feel about the week.

	1	5	10
Progress			
Enjoyment of the Journey			
Feelings of Self-Love			

WRITE NOW! What are your thoughts about this past week? Where did you make progress, and how did it feel?

BUT WHY? In order to keep putting one foot in front of the other on your journey, you have to be motivated. While everyone is motivated by something different, the motivation itself is always central. While ultimately any journey springs from a place of self-love and that keeps you going in a broad sense, you also have something important and specific that motivates you—something about your goal that is special and keeps your fire lit.

WRITE NOW! What is your motivation? What is that special, powerful force that drives you forward?

When something is important enough, you do it even if the odds are not in your favor.

—Elon Musk

Date

Week 10 * Day 2

ICING ON THE CAKE. Besides your big, overarching motivation, there are probably some little perks and nuances relating to your goal that keep you motivated as well. The icing on the cake, so to speak.

WRITE NOW! What ices your cake?

Date

Week 10 * Day 3

NOT JUST YOU. Achieving a goal is not just good for you but for the people around you, and that can be a big motivator.

WRITE NOW! Who around you will benefit from you reaching your goal?

YOUR MOTIVATION. Motivation has been described has a fire, a force, a pull, a drive, a dream, love, fate, and a million other metaphors. It's hard to pin down exactly what motivation is because it's an intangible power that's both the same and different for everyone: a universal that's none-theless personal. While most people just accept motivation as a *thing* without really ever thinking about it, homing in on what motivation feels like to you can help you summon it whenever you're feeling a little low or slow.

WRITE NOW! What does motivation feel like to you? What imagery and emotions does it bring up?

CAN'T LIVE WITHOUT IT. The dream you're trying to realize, that goal you keep pushing toward, is itself, of course, core to your motivation. They are so closely linked that in many ways they are one and the same thing. The fire your goal gives you is an essential element for a rich experience, a life infused with purpose and meaning. To keep going, we have to be going somewhere; otherwise, we founder and stagnate.

WRITE NOW! How has the motivation you feel toward reaching your goal enriched your life?

A dream is a basic need. A dream is as important to the functionality of our life as our breath is to the functioning of our body.

—Sherrie Campbell

PLAY ON. When you're looking to get down to business, there are probably a few songs that really help get you moving—music that gets you off your proverbial rear and sets you in motion.

WRITE NOW! What's on your motivational playlist?

_____

_____

_____

_____

_____

PROGRESS, NOT PERFECTION. Reflect on your journal entries from the past week. Do you feel like you made progress? Do you feel like you enjoyed the journey and showed yourself love and care, or did you get hung up on perfection? Fill in the following progress bars to show how you feel about the week.

	1	5	10
Progress			
Enjoyment of the Journey			
Feelings of Self-Love			

WRITE NOW! What are your thoughts about this past week? Where did you make progress, and how did it feel?

_____

_____

POWER UP. You've been journeying for long enough to have seen your own power at work. Your power to stick to your plan, to do the hard work, to make progress toward your goal. Doubt has undoubtedly crept in from time to time, but instead of letting those thoughts seize power and control, by now you have enough evidence of your strength and perseverance to battle even your biggest doubts. When your thoughts go to that dark place of doubt, you can look back at the progress you've made and see how those doubts don't hold a candle to all that strength you have.

WRITE NOW! What doubts did you start out with that you've seen aren't true?

When you doubt your power,
you give power to your doubts.

—Diane von Furstenberg

FACE YOUR DOUBT. If you want to overcome a lingering doubt, you have to face it head-on. Sometimes a doubt is super specific and sometimes it's a vague shadow beast.

WRITE NOW! Bring any doubts you still have into the light.

DOUBT IT OUT. Now that you've acknowledged that doubt, take it out! See it for the weak-sauce argument that it is and tell it NO!

WRITE NOW! How is that doubt so very, very wrong?

SHUT UP, YOU! OK, that was a little harsh, but sometimes you have to tell that voice inside your head—the one that keeps telling you that you can't, that says you're not good enough, that repeats criticism but forgets praise— to stuff a sock in it! Anyone on a big journey experiences moments, bouts, or even plagues of doubt. Our mind is always trying to problem-solve and protect us, and as such it generates doubt in that process. *If you don't put yourself out there, you can't get hurt,* it thinks. But then you also never get the big wins or reach the big goals, and where's the sense in that?

WRITE NOW! What can you say back to yourself when your mind generates doubt?

BELIEVE IT. Belief that you can do a thing is probably the most powerful force there is. It makes you an unstoppable dynamo that operates under the assumption that you *will*, which keeps you from getting stuck in the swamp of *won't* that is riddled with doubts and maybes and what-ifs. It also means that if you experience a failure or setback, you recognize it as the learning experience it is, instead of the end of the road. That's not to say that if you ever doubt that you will, then you won't. Everyone doubts themselves sometimes, but it's making the choice to believe that you can instead of believing the doubt.

WRITE NOW! Tell the story of how you got to your goal from this moment, operating under the belief that you can—without a doubt—do it.

Doubt kills more dreams than failure ever will.

—Suzy Kassem

TAKE A COMPLIMENT. Most people have the tendency to remember the littlest criticisms and dismiss the highest praise. Let's make an effort to flip that habit.

WRITE NOW! What's the last compliment someone gave you? Bonus points if it relates to your goal.

_____

_____

_____

_____

PROGRESS, NOT PERFECTION. Reflect on your journal entries from the past week. Do you feel like you made progress? Do you feel like you enjoyed the journey and showed yourself love and care, or did you get hung up on perfection? Fill in the following progress bars to show how you feel about the week.

	1	5	10
Progress			
Enjoyment of the Journey			
Feelings of Self-Love			

WRITE NOW! What are your thoughts about this past week? Where did you make progress, and how did it feel?

_____

_____

_____

PICTURE IT. It's next year and you've reached your goal. You're thriving. Things have turned out even better than you first expected, and the future is so bright that you need sunglasses. You're filled with courage and confidence and joy. This scene can be real. In fact, it will be. Visualizing it in great detail will help make it happen because the more real you make it in your mind, the more real it can become in the world.

WRITE NOW! Describe yourself and your life a year from now in great, glorious detail.

See the things you want as already yours.

—Robert Collier

PUT IT UP THERE. Vision boards are collages of images that represent your goal, and they can be tremendously inspiring.

WRITE NOW! What would you put on your vision board? Be as specific as possible. When can you set aside time to make one?

_____

_____

_____

_____

_____

THAT'S AFFIRMATIVE. Vision boards can also include quotes and affirmations that inspire you.

WRITE NOW! What wise words would you put on your vision board?

_____

_____

_____

_____

_____

_____

REHEARSE IT. Just as picturing your goal fully achieved can help you progress on your path toward it, visualizing a tricky step along the way can help you navigate it. If you rehearse in your mind something you're nervous about or unsure of, the better prepared you'll be to meet that challenge. First picture yourself doing whatever it is you have to do, as if you were watching a movie of it, and then step inside yourself and picture doing it from your first-person point of view.

WRITE NOW! Describe your rehearsal in as much detail as you can, bringing in the senses, the scenery, what you're wearing—everything you can to make it feel real.

NOW YOU SEE IT. Now that you have some really clear pictures in mind of your future successful self, and even a tricky step on the way to your goal, you might notice that the path has gotten a little bit brighter and easier to see. Maybe you pictured a detail that inspired you or helped you realize a good step or change in your plan that you hadn't thought of yet.

WRITE NOW! What have you learned from the visualization exercises you practiced this week?

The clearer you are when visualizing your dreams, the brighter the spotlight will be to lead you on the right path.

—Gail Lynne Goodwin

GOT THE HICCUPS? When you were visualizing your goal this week, were there some elements you had a hard time seeing as real? Those are just areas you need to spend more time convincing yourself you can and will. Because you can and will.

WRITE NOW! What were your hiccups?

_____

_____

_____

_____

PROGRESS, NOT PERFECTION Reflect on your journal entries from the past week. Do you feel like you made progress? Do you feel like you enjoyed the journey and showed yourself love and care, or did you get hung up on perfection? Fill in the following progress bars to show how you feel about the week.

	1	5	10
Progress			
Enjoyment of the Journey			
Feelings of Self-Love			

WRITE NOW! What are your thoughts about this past week? Where did you make progress, and how did it feel?

_____

_____

YOU'RE DOING IT! You're a quarter of a way through your year of progress—congratulations! No matter what the journey has been like so far—if you've loved it or hated it or both loved *and* hated it—you should take a moment to pat yourself on the back for sticking with your plan to reach your goal. That commitment is the key ingredient of any success story. Because while you probably have wished for something like a movie montage to get you through the hard work from time to time, pushing to reach each step of the journey is what creates a champion.

WRITE NOW! Reflect on your journey as a whole so far.

_____

_____

_____

_____

_____

_____

_____

_____

_____

*I hated every minute of training, but I said,
"Don't quit. Suffer now and live the rest
of your life as a champion."*

—Muhammad Ali

HARD FEELINGS. There *are* going to be moments when you feel like quitting; understanding those hard feelings is important to overcoming them

WRITE NOW! When have you felt like quitting?

STRONG FEELINGS. If you're here, that means you didn't quit, and that's amazing! You're strong and growing stronger still.

WRITE NOW! What did it feel like when you resisted the urge to quit?

ROLL WITH IT. No journey, no matter how well mapped, comes without its surprises. Sometimes good, sometimes not so good, and sometimes unqualifiable, the bumps, twists, and turns you experience on the path to your goal not only keep things interesting, but they can teach you things about yourself and sometimes even reshape your path. Maybe you'll learn that you have a strength you never knew about and you want to rewrite your goal to play to it. Or maybe something you thought was super important turns out to be overhyped.

WRITE NOW! What surprises have you experienced on your journey? How have they impacted your goal?

REVISITING AND REVISING. It can be helpful to revisit your plan to see where you're at and if you want to make any changes. Go back to week 2 and see where you are in the overall plan and what step you're currently on. Is the plan working for you? Has your goal changed? If so, in what ways?

WRITE NOW! Revise your plan to play to any strengths you've discovered and changes you've made to your goal.

To improve is to change; to be perfect is to have changed often.

—Winston Churchill

I DO. Recommitting to your journey and your goal every so often can reinvigorate you. It revitalizes your enthusiasm and reminds you what all the work is for.

WRITE NOW! In a few words, recommit to your plan and your goal.

_____

_____

_____

_____

_____

PROGRESS, NOT PERFECTION. Reflect on your journal entries from the past week. Do you feel like you made progress? Do you feel like you enjoyed the journey and showed yourself love and care, or did you get hung up on perfection? Fill in the following progress bars to show how you feel about the week.

	1	5	10
Progress			
Enjoyment of the Journey			
Feelings of Self-Love			

WRITE NOW! What are your thoughts about this past week? Where did you make progress, and how did it feel?

_____

_____

KICK IT UP A NOTCH. It's time to take things to the next level! Whether you've been feeling like you're on a plateau or making good progress, deciding that you're going to kick it into the next gear is sure to motivate some positive change. The next level might mean tackling the next big step in your plan, doing an intimidating thing you've been reluctant to try, or reaching a milestone. Whatever it is, it's time to do it!

WRITE NOW! What's the "next level" for you? And what do you need to do to get there?

If you always do what you've always done, you always get what you've always gotten.

—attributed to Jessie Potter

RISK. Usually getting to the next level means taking some kind of risk, and often that risk involves facing the potential disappointment of not succeeding in your first attempt.

WRITE NOW! What is the biggest risk you face in getting to the next level?

_____

_____

_____

_____

_____

REWARD. As the old saying goes, nothing ventured nothing gained.

WRITE NOW! What do you stand to gain by taking the risk?

_____

_____

_____

_____

_____

_____

READ ALL ABOUT IT. Researching your goal can help you gain invaluable insight into what it takes to get there. Knowing as much as you can about what you're doing and how other people have gotten there in the past serves as both road map and inspiration. By arming yourself with an education on your goal, you can avoid (or at least plan for) obstacles. Instead of reinventing the wheel, you can take someone else's blueprints for it and make the wheel that best helps you roll along.

WRITE NOW! What about your goal would you like to research? Where will you go for resources?

UPFRONT COST. When you're devoted to progress toward a goal, that can often mean some sacrifice. It might be that you have to give up your spare time or that you have to push yourself out of your comfort zone or that you have to sacrifice luxuries you once enjoyed. Whatever that upfront cost is, and no matter how hard it is to pay it, reaching your goal and progressing into the person you want to become are the kinds of rewards that make all the effort worth it.

WRITE NOW! What sacrifices have you made or are you thinking of making for your goal?

_____

_____

_____

_____

_____

_____

_____

_____

_____

_____

I need to have a purpose in life and for that I might sacrifice some of the luxuries that I enjoy.

—Margot Fonteyn

DON'T LISTEN. There are always people in the world who will tell you that you can't do something. Their own crappy opinions are their problem, though, not yours.

WRITE NOW! Who should you stop listening to when it comes to chasing your dream?

_____

_____

_____

_____

PROGRESS, NOT PERFECTION. Reflect on your journal entries from the past week. Do you feel like you made progress? Do you feel like you enjoyed the journey and showed yourself love and care, or did you get hung up on perfection? Fill in the following progress bars to show how you feel about the week.

	1	5	10
Progress			
Enjoyment of the Journey			
Feelings of Self-Love			

WRITE NOW! What are your thoughts about this past week? Where did you make progress, and how did it feel?

_____

_____

WE CAN ALL BE HEROES. Some people in the world seem superhuman. What they've accomplished, their influence, how brilliant they are—it just doesn't seem possible that an ordinary person could be that amazing. But the truth is, each and every one of them is just an ordinary person who decided to be extraordinary and put in the work. You can do it, too; you're already on your way.

WRITE NOW! Who are your heroes, and what do you admire about them?

All the best heroes are ordinary people who make themselves extraordinary.

—Gerard Way

SUPER PEOPLE. Every journey has a step that seems like it requires super-powers to take. Yet, if you look around, you'll probably notice lots of people who've surmounted similar challenges.

WRITE NOW! Who do you know who could take that daunting step?

➡

_____

_____

_____

_____

_____

STEP UP. Admiring the accomplishments of other people can sometimes show you what you need to do or work on to take your next big step.

WRITE NOW! What is the trait or belief you think others have that allows them to take the big steps?

➡

_____

_____

_____

_____

_____

THE OLD YOU. When you look back at your younger self, you probably can recall some things you've done that you can't imagine doing now. OK, sure, for some of them you can't believe how naive or foolish you were. (We've all got those; they're called "learning experiences.") For others, you probably can't believe how brave or strong or determined you were. Sometimes the impetuousness of youth can yield big rewards because you don't even consider how hard a thing is—you just do it.

WRITE NOW! What are some triumphs the old you had? Are there any traits you used to have that you want to dust off and bring back?

YOUR OWN HERO. It's easy to look around and become awed by other people and all they've accomplished. People have done so many wonderful and wild things in this world. Looking to others to see what they've done can be intimidating, but it can also be a source of great strength if you remember that they're just people, too. Seeing what they've done can serve as a reminder that you're capable of great feats, too. It's terrific to have heroes to look up to, but it's even better when you feel like you can look at them on the same level.

WRITE NOW! What qualities do you admire in others that you want to grow in yourself?

In this life you have to be your own hero.

—Jeanette Winterson

DON'T BE MODEST. Throw away all modesty and think about some of the amazing things you've done.

WRITE NOW! When have you been your own hero?

_____

_____

_____

_____

_____

PROGRESS, NOT PERFECTION. Reflect on your journal entries from the past week. Do you feel like you made progress? Do you feel like you enjoyed the journey and showed yourself love and care, or did you get hung up on perfection? Fill in the following progress bars to show how you feel about the week.

	1	5	10
Progress			
Enjoyment of the Journey			
Feelings of Self-Love			

WRITE NOW! What are your thoughts about this past week? Where did you make progress, and how did it feel?

_____

_____

GIVE IT A REST. Making progress toward your goal can get addictive. You feel so good striding along that you keep pushing yourself and pushing yourself. Maybe sometimes that means you keep going even when you're tired. While that's not a bad thing in itself, it is important to know the difference between wanting to take a break and *needing* to take a break. As we saw on week 5, day 6, giving yourself rest and recovery time is critical to any long-term endeavor if you want to make it to your goal without burning out or getting hurt.

WRITE NOW! How do you treat rest? Do you resist it or embrace it?

Rest can come, even while there is more work to do.

—Rachel Kang

IT'S ALL ABOUT YOU. We all have our favorite rest rituals, the shows we binge-watch, or the foods we eat when we need a break.

WRITE NOW! When you need to relax and take a break, how do you treat it like a ritual?

_____

_____

_____

_____

_____

SOUNDS RELAXING. Music and soundscapes make great aids when you're trying to unwind.

WRITE NOW! What do you like to listen to when you're trying to rest and relax?

_____

_____

_____

_____

_____

SLEEP HABITS. Routinely getting good sleep helps just about everything in life. From stamina to focus to acuity to just feeling good instead of snippy and irritated, being well rested is the cornerstone of it all. New research shows that the ideal bedtime for optimum health is between 10 and 11 p.m. Putting one foot in front of the other on your journey of progress is made that much easier when you're getting solid sleep. If you're not, you probably will start dragging before too long. While sleep is easy for some people, other people have to work on getting a good night's rest.

WRITE NOW! What are your sleep habits like? Is there anything you can do to get better sleep?

REAL REST. Rest doesn't mean just sleep or just inactivity. Real rest is putting down your burdens, putting down your drive, putting down even the ideas of progress and goals to just be. If you're technically being still but you're still going over your plans and goals in your head, you're not really resting. If this is you, you may need to try some advanced resting techniques like meditating, aimless walking, mindful crafting, or taking an honest-to-goodness vacation.

WRITE NOW! What will you do to ensure that you'll get some real downtime?

Each person deserves a day away, in which no problems are confronted, no solutions reached for. Each of us needs to withdraw from the cares which will not withdraw from us.

—Maya Angelou

PLAYTIME. Play is another kind of rest, and arguably it's the most fun kind.

WRITE NOW! What are your favorite ways to play?

PROGRESS, NOT PERFECTION. Reflect on your journal entries from the past week. Do you feel like you made progress? Do you feel like you enjoyed the journey and showed yourself love and care, or did you get hung up on perfection? Fill in the following progress bars to show how you feel about the week.

	1	5	10
Progress			
Enjoyment of the Journey			
Feelings of Self-Love			

WRITE NOW! What are your thoughts about this past week? Where did you make progress, and how did it feel?

FEEL THE FEAR. When fear sets in—fear of failure, of not being perfect, of what others will think, or of something more visceral like pain—most likely your first instinct is to run, to avoid the pain, to protect yourself. That response has kept people alive for millennia by helping them escape and avoid deadly dangers. But in our modern world, most of the time the things we fear aren't predators with big teeth, but our brain still responds as if they were. If we overcome that impulse to run from fear, it can become a guiding force that shines light on what's really important. After all, if it weren't important, you wouldn't be so afraid.

WRITE NOW! What are your big fears about your journey?

Fear is a light that's meant to guide us.
It builds strength and provides sustenance.

—Meera Lee Patel

ORIGIN STORY. Our fears come from somewhere, whether from a childhood event or a lesson learned later in life.

WRITE NOW! Where did your biggest fear come from?

_____

_____

_____

_____

_____

_____

FIRST FEAR. After you become afraid of something, that fear can become a recurring motif in your life.

WRITE NOW! When have you had a big run-in with your fear?

_____

_____

_____

_____

_____

_____

FROM FEAR TO FIERCE. Facing a fear is one of the ultimate character-building experiences you can have. And it's one that is likely necessary to take some of the big steps on your journey. You gain so much strength from overcoming something that terrifies you, and that strength allows you to throw open more and more doors, so you can do more and greater things than you once thought possible. You begin to think things like *Well, if I can do that, I can do anything* as you stride toward your goal. That confidence makes the road clearer and easier to travel, leveling what once seemed like mountains into manageable and even enjoyable terrain.

WRITE NOW! What fears have you faced in your past? What did you learn from them?

THE FEAR FACT. While facing your fears can make you strong and take you to great places, doing so doesn't eliminate fear. Fear is a fact of life. There will always be something you're afraid of, and that's OK. It's just another opportunity to grow and get stronger. Once you accept that fear will always be there, you might just find that your fears' claws aren't quite so sharp anymore. Sure, there's stuff to be afraid of—that's life. But you're brave and strong, and you're going to keep going anyway into the great unknown.

WRITE NOW! What is a fear you want to face? How will go you about slaying it?

---

*I have accepted fear as part of life. . . .
I have gone ahead despite the pounding in
the heart that says: turn back, turn back.*

—Erica Jong

NAME YOUR FEAR. Sometimes naming and even personifying a fear can help you fight it. If you pretend that it's an imaginary frenemy, then you can tell it to shut up and go away.

WRITE NOW! Name and describe one of your fears.

_____

_____

_____

_____

_____

PROGRESS, NOT PERFECTION. Reflect on your journal entries from the past week. Do you feel like you made progress? Do you feel like you enjoyed the journey and showed yourself love and care, or did you get hung up on perfection? Fill in the following progress bars to show how you feel about the week.

	1	5	10
Progress			
Enjoyment of the Journey			
Feelings of Self-Love			

WRITE NOW! What are your thoughts about this past week? Where did you make progress, and how did it feel?

_____

_____

PRACTICE, NOT PERFECTION The saying goes that practice makes perfect, and while we know that perfection isn't really a thing, practice is the means by which you reach your goals. It's the work you do to get better and better and closer and closer to where you want to be, but that work is never done. Musicians don't practice until they reach a certain level of proficiency and then stop playing. Doctors don't practice medicine until they cure a certain number of patients and then call it a day. Practice is the process of creating your self.

WRITE NOW! What are you practicing to get you closer to your goal?

I am a soul in process. I am life in the making. I am a weaver with shuttle and thread, and back in my loom the design begins to show.

—Muriel Strode

PAST PRACTICES. When we're children, repetitive activities like doing homework, participating in sports, and playing instruments teach us the art of practicing.

WRITE NOW! What's something you've enjoyed practicing in your life?

_____

_____

_____

_____

_____

LESSONS LEARNED. By practicing you gain confidence, knowledge, and new skills that carry over beyond the activity itself.

WRITE NOW! What lessons have you learned from practicing?

_____

_____

_____

_____

_____

BEST PRACTICES. As with most things in life, there are many ways to practice and some will suit you better than others. You may prefer working on an individual part of an activity until you become proficient at it. Or maybe you'd rather work on a different part every day or the whole thing at once or the part you really enjoy or the part that needs the most work. You might do all of these, depending on your mood and what you want to achieve. All these ways are valid and the only thing that matters is what works for you.

WRITE NOW! What does your practice method look like?

PRACTICE GREATNESS. While there is such a thing as being born with natural talent, it's generally of no use without practice. On the other side of the coin, just because you are not innately good at something doesn't mean you cannot become good at it through practice. There are probably aspects of your journey that will come easily and others you will have to work harder at. Practice is essential for both. Your greatness comes from the work you put in.

WRITE NOW! What's something you could practice more to get to your goal?

Excellence is an art won by training and habituation; we do not act rightly because we have virtue or excellence, but we rather have these because we have acted rightly.

—Will Durant

FIVE-MINUTE RULE. There will, of course, be times when you don't feel like practicing at all. Commit to just five short minutes of practice right now and see where you get.

WRITE NOW! How did your five minutes of practice turn out?

_____   _____

_____

_____

_____

_____

PROGRESS, NOT PERFECTION. Reflect on your journal entries from the past week. Do you feel like you made progress? Do you feel like you enjoyed the journey and showed yourself love and care, or did you get hung up on perfection? Fill in the following progress bars to show how you feel about the week.

	1	5	10
Progress			
Enjoyment of the Journey			
Feelings of Self-Love			

WRITE NOW! What are your thoughts about this past week? Where did you make progress, and how did it feel?

_____

_____

DON'T GET DERAILED. You're human and one of the conditions of being human is that you'll inevitably come up against some kind of setback. You'll be chugging right along and all of a sudden you'll get a track change or a stop signal and then you're just sitting there. Maybe you're even going backward a bit. That sort of thing is as inevitable as a sunrise. The trick is not to become derailed by it. See it for the inevitability that it is and, if you can, try to learn from it.

WRITE NOW! What setbacks or backsliding have you experienced on your journey? What have you learned from that?

Keep your eyes on the stars, but don't forget that your feet are necessarily on the earth.

—Theodore Roosevelt

LOOK OUT AHEAD! Early detection of things that are likely to derail you can help you set up a detour.

WRITE NOW! What sort of things set you back or get you offtrack?

FIND AN ALTERNATE ROUTE. Now that you've identified potential problems, you can plan around them.

WRITE NOW! How can you get around the things that typically derail you?

BE GENTLE. When you've hit a setback and maybe taken a step or two back, it's tempting to start beating up on yourself. However, this is a time that requires understanding and self-compassion. You've worked so hard and come so far and the inevitable setback does nothing to diminish that. Obviously, something difficult is going on, so instead of being hard on yourself, be gentle. It's just another part of the process that you can embrace and get great at.

WRITE NOW! What will you do to show yourself some gentle care when you're experiencing a hard time or a setback?

AN HONEST MISTAKE. Sometimes setbacks and mistakes are caused by pushing too far forward when you're not quite ready. You bump up against a limitation, and it knocks you back a bit. This kind of small failure can be a nonevent, or it can cause you to spiral out of control. To keep things in perspective and not mistake a temporary limitation for a permanent barrier, take a step back and evaluate what's going on. Try to determine if you've been pushing too hard so you can honestly see where you are and what you need to do.

WRITE NOW! Are you pushing too hard in some area? Is there something that might be better served by slowing down instead of speeding up?

Don't make a tragedy of a simple failure. Study your capabilities first, and if you have overrated their strength, try again, going more slowly.

—Minna Thomas Antrim

HINDSIGHT IS 20/20. Failures are just lessons wearing brass knuckles. They beat you up a bit, but the point is to learn by looking back on them.

WRITE NOW! If you had the chance to try again at something you've failed at, what would you do differently?

_____

_____

_____

_____

_____

PROGRESS, NOT PERFECTION. Reflect on your journal entries from the past week. Do you feel like you made progress? Do you feel like you enjoyed the journey and showed yourself love and care, or did you get hung up on perfection? Fill in the following progress bars to show how you feel about the week.

	1	5	10
Progress			
Enjoyment of the Journey			
Feelings of Self-Love			

WRITE NOW! What are your thoughts about this past week? Where did you make progress, and how did it feel?

_____

_____

LITTLE WINS COUNT. When you're on a big journey with your eyes locked on your goal, it can be easy to overlook all the little wins you have achieved along the way. Slow improvements, incremental change, even just sticking with the plan are all wins that you might not even notice if the voice in your head is still going on and on, criticizing your progress and whispering that you really should be perfect by now. You can shut that little critic up by taking note of your small victories.

WRITE NOW! What are some of the small wins you've had on your journey?

Small wins can be easy to gloss over, especially if you've been raised on a diet of self-criticism and perfectionism.

—Tess Miller

THOUGHTS COUNT. Changing the way you think from *I can't* to *I can* or blocking old judgments and thinking more positively are big wins.

WRITE NOW! How have your thoughts changed during your journey?

_____

_____

_____

_____

_____

_____

PLAN A PARTY. There are lots of ways to celebrate little wins you've had—a special treat, a favorite activity, a little song and dance.

WRITE NOW! Pick a win you're really proud of and plan a celebration for it here.

_____

_____

_____

_____

_____

_____

CELEBRATE, MOTIVATE. One of the best reasons to celebrate little victories is that doing so energizes you and gives you the motivation to keep going. If you're just waiting for that big day when all your dreams come true, you're missing a whole lot of life and adventure. As we've said, the goal isn't the only thing of worth; the journey itself is so very valuable. All the little improvements and wins you have as you go along make the journey a joy and keep it from becoming a slog.

WRITE NOW! What is the last little victory you had? How did (or will) you celebrate it?

LINKS IN A CHAIN. Reaching a goal isn't just a single moment in time. It's the crowning jewel on a necklace made of beautiful links that each have value and add to the beauty of the whole. Each link is a win you had, a skill you gained, an obstacle you overcame. They're all the work you did to get somewhere you really wanted to go.

WRITE NOW! What are the links in your chain of success so far?

Your success is a series of small wins.

—Jamie Tardy

FEEL THAT? This week has been all about focusing on the wins and successes you've had already. Now it's time to reflect on that positive momentum you've created and sum it all up.

WRITE NOW! How does it feel to win?

_____

_____

_____

_____

_____

PROGRESS NOT PERFECTION. Reflect on your journal entries from the past week. Do you feel like you made progress? Do you feel like you enjoyed the journey and showed yourself love and care, or did you get hung up on perfection? Fill in the following progress bars to show how you feel about the week.

	1	5	10
Progress			
Enjoyment of the Journey			
Feelings of Self-Love			

WRITE NOW! What are your thoughts about this past week? Where did you make progress, and how did it feel?

_____

_____

STEP BY STEP. The act of doing, taking step after step on your journey, will get you where you want to go. It's the simplest truth, but it's also one of the hardest things to do. Being persistent—showing up day after day; keeping on trying, even when you're scared or feel like quitting or are disheartened or just stumbled—can take everything you've got sometimes. But if your dream is big enough, then doesn't it make sense for you to give it all you've got?

WRITE NOW! Who do you admire for their persistence? What have they accomplished with it, and what has that taught you?

_My most important talent
—or habit—was "persistence."_

—Octavia Butler

GETTING THERE. Showing up can be one of the hardest things to do, and that doesn't just apply to the start of the journey. It applies to restarting your journey each day.

WRITE NOW! What's the hardest thing about showing up sometimes?

WORTH IT. When something is really hard, when you really have to work, kicking butt feels even better.

WRITE NOW! How do you feel after you push through and show up anyway?

WHEN THE TANK IS LOW. Another truth about persistence is that you don't have to—and can't—always give it your all. Sometimes you show up and you just don't have it. That's fine. Do what you can, even if it's not much. Then recognize that your tank is low, think of something fun and caring that will fill it up, and be super proud that you showed up at all. That's one of the hardest things to pull off. But sticking to your goal through thick and thin is what gets you there.

WRITE NOW! Write a letter of congratulations to yourself for showing up, even when you don't feel like it.

BIGGER CHALLENGES, BETTER YOU. The way you grow, the way you get to your goal, is by tackling bigger and bigger challenges. Your journey probably started out with some light lifting, but once you're in the thick of it, really doing the work, the challenges get bigger, but so do your strides. The challenges grow because you've gotten better and better and can take on more and more. Sometimes those challenges may beat you back a step or two at first, but, if you persist, you'll beat them and grow even stronger.

WRITE NOW! How have the challenges you face on your journey gotten harder? How have you grown to meet them?

*For growth is profoundly conquered to be
By ever greater things.*

—Rainer Maria Rilke

PERSISTENCE IS POETRY IN MOTION. Haikus are traditional Japanese poems consisting of three lines that are always five, seven, and five syllables. They attempt to condense a lot of meaning into very few words.

WRITE NOW! Try your hand at creating a haiku about your persistence.

_____

_____

_____

_____

_____

PROGRESS, NOT PERFECTION. Reflect on your journal entries from the past week. Do you feel like you made progress? Do you feel like you enjoyed the journey and showed yourself love and care, or did you get hung up on perfection? Fill in the following progress bars to show how you feel about the week.

	1	5	10
Progress			
Enjoyment of the Journey			
Feelings of Self-Love			

WRITE NOW! What are your thoughts about this past week? Where did you make progress, and how did it feel?

_____

_____

GROWING PAINS. As you progress on your journey, you'll change and grow, and that growth may be painful. It requires a great amount of trust in yourself and the work required to take control of your life and then keep it. This can mean ignoring the well-meaning advice of friends and loved ones, taking risks, and making sacrifices.

WRITE NOW! What growing pains have you experienced on your journey?

_____

_____

_____

_____

_____

_____

_____

Growth ain't for weenies, but it's nowhere near as painful as living the life you're living right now if you're not REALLY going for it. If you want to take control of your life ... stop at nothing. Have faith. Trust that your new life is already here and is far better than the old.

—Jen Sincero

WHAT YOU CAN CONTROL. Sometimes a big challenge is recognizing what you have control over—things you have always believed were beyond you.

WRITE NOW! What might you take control over on your journey that you've always felt was beyond your grasp?

_____

_____

_____

_____

_____

WHAT YOU CAN'T CONTROL. The other big challenge is recognizing things that you can't control, no matter how much you want to.

WRITE NOW! What aspects of your journey are outside your control?

_____

_____

_____

_____

_____

WISE WORDS. It's said that real wisdom is, at least in part, recognizing what you can't control but then controlling how you react to those things. In other words, there is not much in the world that you can control and your reactions and actions are some of the only things you have power over. You may not control much, but you can control yourself. The real challenge and triumph is understanding this and acting accordingly. Understand what's out of your control—whether they be obstacles, irritations, or downright infuriating circumstances—and control how you respond them. This means not getting upset or raging or feeling defeated and, instead, accepting and reacting in the best way you can.

WRITE NOW! How do you want to respond to the parts of your journey that are outside your control?

STEERING THE SHIP. Even though much of the world is beyond your control, being in control of yourself is enormously gratifying and powerful. It takes real work to know yourself and act accordingly, to steer your ship toward the horizon you want instead of allowing the winds of other people's opinions to blow you off course or to take in the sails and just drift along with the current. The reward is nothing less than a full life well lived.

WRITE NOW! How has it felt taking control of your ship over these past few months? What have you learned?

No one saves us but ourselves.

—Buddha

KNOWING THE DIFFERENCE. This week was all about reflecting on what you control and what you don't so you can feel confident in what you control and let go of what you don't.

WRITE NOW! Are you still fighting to control things beyond your control or vice versa?

_____

_____   _____

_____   _____

_____

PROGRESS, NOT PERFECTION. Reflect on your journal entries from the past week. Do you feel like you made progress? Do you feel like you enjoyed the journey and showed yourself love and care, or did you get hung up on perfection? Fill in the following progress bars to show how you feel about the week.

	1	5	10
Progress			
Enjoyment of the Journey			
Feelings of Self-Love			

WRITE NOW! What are your thoughts about this past week? Where did you make progress, and how did it feel?

_____

_____

FEEL THE FLOW. Is there anything better than being in the flow? When you're doing something you love, sometimes everything else falls away and you become pure action, pure doing. It is like being in a higher state. It's often characterized as being "in the zone." As you get farther and farther along on your journey, you might experience flow more frequently. As you practice and get better at the work it takes to reach your goal, it's likely that you get into the flow of that work. This experience is a reward in and of itself. It's the joy of the journey.

WRITE NOW! When do you experience flow?

_____

_____

_____

_____

_____

_____

_____

_____

*"Flow"—the state in which people
are so involved in an activity
that nothing else seems to matter.*

—Mihaly Csikszentmihalyi

BIG AND SMALL. You can be in the flow while practicing a concerto or painting a portrait, but you can also be in the flow doing something simple, like crunches or organizing your space.

WRITE NOW! What little things do you do that bring on a state of flow?

_____

_____

_____

_____

_____

_____

MORE FLOW. Now that you've thought about when you're in the flow, perhaps you've noticed some things you can do to get into that state more often.

WRITE NOW! What can you do to bring more flow into your journey?

_____

_____

_____

_____

_____

DEFINE YOUR FLOW. Flow has been described many different ways. Some people call it the merging of thought and action, others talk about it as a forgetting of self-consciousness or self-awareness. It's been described as the state of pure being or full immersion, of riding the life force of the universe. People have described it as channeling angels or other higher powers—an idea sometimes taken quite literally, especially in the medieval period. Flow is one of those funny things that's personal yet universal; it's something we all relish and enjoy. We all experience it, and yet we all have something different to say about it.

WRITE NOW! Describe flow in your own words.

FIND YOUR FLOW. Just like everyone has their own way of describing flow, different things bring on flow for different people. It's not about doing what works for other people, it's about finding what works for you. This is especially true when it comes to the work you're doing on your journey. The steps you've chosen to take are undoubtedly steps that have worked for other people and while they may be working for you, too, it's always good to take a deeper look and see if you can change anything to better suit your own style.

WRITE NOW! Is there some step on your journey that you really don't like? Was that step prescribed to you somehow? Is there something different you could do that you'd like more and might even get you into a flow state?

Go with the flow. Force nothing. Let it happen, or not happen ... trusting that whichever way it goes, it's for the best.

—Mandy Hale

FOSTERING FLOW. Flow is often achieved when you do something that's somewhat hard but that you feel confident and capable about. It's reaching for that next step or stage of the journey.

WRITE NOW! What's the next step you feel capable of reaching?

_____

_____

_____

_____

_____

PROGRESS, NOT PERFECTION. Reflect on your journal entries from the past week. Do you feel like you made progress? Do you feel like you enjoyed the journey and showed yourself love and care, or did you get hung up on perfection? Fill in the following progress bars to show how you feel about the week.

	1	5	10
Progress			
Enjoyment of the Journey			
Feelings of Self-Love			

WRITE NOW! What are your thoughts about this past week? Where did you make progress, and how did it feel?

_____

_____

A BABY STEP. There are times in a journey when you're ready to make a huge push. You're energized, you have a plan, you're primed and eager to go! Then there are other times when you are hanging onto your motivation by nothing but a slim thread and just about any task feels daunting. That's when it's time for a baby step—a tiny movement forward that doesn't have to be graceful and very well may end up with a tumble but, hey, it's still a step!

WRITE NOW! What are some tiny steps you can take toward your goal, even on days when you're really not feeling it?

Mistakes are necessary! Stumbles are normal. These are baby steps. Progress, not perfection, is what we should be asking of ourselves.

—Julia Cameron

RETAIL THERAPY. Buying a new piece of equipment or a tool or whatever can be a fun boost to flagging motivation.

WRITE NOW! What is something you've been meaning to get to help you on your journey?

_____

_____

_____

_____

_____

THIS COUNTS. Every action you take associated with your goal is progress, including filling out this journal.

WRITE NOW! What other small actions do you regularly take toward your goal that you haven't counted toward your progress but, in fact, are part of the journey?

_____

_____

_____

_____

_____

FOR THE FUN OF IT. Not every aspect of progress has to be—or should be—hard work. Some things that get you closer to your goal are probably fun or otherwise enjoyable in their own way. Whether the joy comes from a sense of accomplishment, a feeling of flow, or from simply loving what you're doing, focusing on that fun and positivity keeps you motivated and moving forward. This is especially important to think about when you're feeling stuck on a plateau or otherwise stymied on your journey.

WRITE NOW! What's a fun or enjoyable part of the progress you're making?

SLOW AND STEADY. *Kaizen* is a Japanese philosophy of incremental improvement and change. In the United States, this idea has become popular in business management, but it's finding its way into the mainstream as well, because it is a simple and beautiful philosophy. You can make great changes by taking your time and slowly going where you want to go. In this way, you can be passionate every day without putting so much pressure on yourself that you burn out.

WRITE NOW! What do you think about *kaizen*? If you want to, how can you bring it into your journey?

The term "kaizen" refers to incremental progress toward your goal. . . . You can take the first small step toward your dream today and keep taking small steps to grow your passions every day after.

—Marie Kondo

SCHEDULE IT. Putting something on the calendar and giving yourself a deadline is especially motivating for some people.

WRITE NOW! What's a next step you want to achieve, and when do you want it done?

_____

_____

_____

_____

_____

PROGRESS, NOT PERFECTION. Reflect on your journal entries from the past week. Do you feel like you made progress? Do you feel like you enjoyed the journey and showed yourself love and care, or did you get hung up on perfection? Fill in the following progress bars to show how you feel about the week.

	1	5	10
Progress			
Enjoyment of the Journey			
Feelings of Self-Love			

WRITE NOW! What are your thoughts about this past week? Where did you make progress, and how did it feel?

_____

_____

THE DIFFERENCE. While your journey may be long and challenging, when you're working toward a goal you care about, that work tends to feel good, or at least satisfying. Doing something you're passionate about may be hard, but it's the kind of hard that motivates and gets you out of bed in the morning, instead of giving you the Sunday-night blues people get before another long week doing work they don't feel good about or personally connected to. As you're striding toward your goal, it's good to tune in to how you're feeling about the work.

WRITE NOW! How have you felt about the work lately? Are you feeling passionate, or are you getting stressed out?

Working hard for something we don't care about is called stress. Working hard for something we love is called passion.

—Simon Sinek

FIRST PLACE. If you're feeling burned out or stressed by the journey, you can revisit the core reason you're doing all this work in the first place: your goal and why it's important to you.

WRITE NOW! What aspect of your goal are you most passionate about?

_____

_____

_____

_____

_____

_____

COUNT IT. Looking back on your progress is another good way to rekindle passion.

WRITE NOW! What have you achieved on your journey so far that you're super proud of?

_____

_____

_____

_____

CHANGE IT UP. You're the author of your journey, and, as such, you can do things however you like. If you find something about the work you're doing particularly stressful, consider backing off from it for a while. You may find that it's not a necessary step on your journey, or, if it is, maybe there's another way you can go about it. Or maybe you'll be better prepared to deal with it farther down the path. What you don't want to do is turn something you're passionate about into something you dread.

WRITE NOW! What's stressing you out or just too difficult to handle at the moment? Make a plan that skips it for now and comes back to it later, if needed.

_____

_____

_____

_____

_____

_____

_____

_____

_____

_____

_____

REAL ABUNDANCE. When you work toward a goal you feel passionate about, when you're doing what you love—even if it's not your full-time occupation—your cup will stay full. That's the key to a fulfilled life. It's not material wealth or ample time to do nothing. Those things may be nice, but if you want to feel fulfilled, and have an abundance of energy and joy and love, progress is the key. It's the feeling of getting better and better and moving closer and closer to something you cherish.

WRITE NOW! What do you have an abundance of in your life?

Doing what you love is the cornerstone of having abundance in your life.

—Wayne W. Dyer

ONE LITTLE THING. It's said that just a small positive thought in the morning can change your whole day.

WRITE NOW! What positive thought do you want to start your day with?

_____

_____

_____

_____

_____

PROGRESS, NOT PERFECTION. Reflect on your journal entries from the past week. Do you feel like you made progress? Do you feel like you enjoyed the journey and showed yourself love and care, or did you get hung up on perfection? Fill in the following progress bars to show how you feel about the week.

	1	5	10
Progress			
Enjoyment of the Journey			
Feelings of Self-Love			

WRITE NOW! What are your thoughts about this past week? Where did you make progress, and how did it feel?

_____

_____

HALFWAY THERE! This week marks the midway point on your journey, and that is truly amazing! You should feel an immense amount of pride for working so hard and sticking to your goal. There were likely some precarious ups and downs, and times you felt like tucking this journal in a drawer and forgetting about the whole darn thing. But you didn't, and that right there is an immense part of the challenge and a critical element of success. Progress, like most things, can be made into a habit just by doing it often enough.

WRITE NOW! Congratulate yourself on getting halfway through this year-long journey.

Just showing up is half the battle.

—Modern proverb

WHO KNEW? Just when you think something is going to be a snap, that step turns out to be a trapdoor into a real obstacle.

WRITE NOW! When in the past six months did something end up being harder than you thought it would be? How did you triumph over it?

SURPRISE! Sometimes dreaded steps turn out to be much easier than you thought, once you get started. You feared them for a long time and then they were a breeze.

WRITE NOW! When was something easier than you thought it would be?

HIGH POINTS. While there were surely moments on the first half of your journey when you felt like quitting, there also had to be moments you felt like a badass winning machine. Times when you felt amazing about the work you were doing, when you were in the zone, could do no wrong, and were super proud of what you were accomplishing. (That's not to say your mind didn't feed you some self-doubt later on, but, as we've learned, that's just what our inner critic does and we can ignore that voice.) Those fist-pump moments are critical. While you're heading toward a goal, it's those high points on the journey that make going after the goal worth it.

WRITE NOW! Describe what it feels like to be a super-charged butt kicker.

DOWNHILL IN A GOOD WAY. Now that you're halfway through, you can feel pretty confident that you're going to get to your goal. Starting is often the hardest part of any journey, and you've more than started—you started and kept at it. And keeping at it, showing up day after day, is the second hardest part—and you've won that battle and turned progress into a daily habit. You know you can get to your goal because you've proved that you've got what it takes. While the rest of the journey might not be an easy downhill coast, you've already done most of the hard peddling.

WRITE NOW! What do you think the second half of your journey will be like?

_____

_____

_____

_____

_____

_____

_____

_____

_____

_____

Once you're halfway home, you know that you can probably get the rest of the way there.

—attributed to Janis Ian

LOOKING FORWARD. With much of the groundwork behind you, some exciting steps await you in your near future.

WRITE NOW! What upcoming step are you really looking forward to?

_____

_____

_____

_____

_____

PROGRESS NOT PERFECTION. Reflect on your journal entries from the past week. Do you feel like you made progress? Do you feel like you enjoyed the journey and showed yourself love and care, or did you get hung up on perfection? Fill in the following progress bars to show how you feel about the week.

	1	5	10
Progress			
Enjoyment of the Journey			
Feelings of Self-Love			

WRITE NOW! What are your thoughts about this past week? Where did you make progress, and how did it feel?

_____

_____

SELF-TALK. Becoming aware of your thoughts and the way you talk to yourself is an incredibly revealing experience. For instance, when you walk past a mirror, are you complimentary or more likely to say something mean? When you think about your progress and your goal, are you dismissive of the work you've done and your chances of success, or do you feel proud and confident? Our culture promotes the idea that we should come down hard on ourselves: If we're not hyper-aware of and exaggerating our foibles, we're self-deluding egomaniacs. But that kind of perpetual harshness can rob you of well-deserved confidence that can help you make real progress.

WRITE NOW! What's your self-talk like?

You must learn a new way to think before you can master a new way to be.

—Marianne Williamson

OBJECTION! OVERRULED. It's easy to make negative thoughts a habit, but if you recognize them when they crop up, you can object to them and eventually overrule them.

WRITE NOW! What's a negative thought or doubt you often have about your goal? Come up with a quick phrase—like "Overruled!"—that you can say to yourself when that thought appears.

_____

_____

_____

_____

_____

CASE DISMISSED! One way to dismiss self-doubt or self-criticism is to put the thought on trial and prove that it's not true.

WRITE NOW! What's something you beat yourself up about? Why is that doubt or criticism untrue?

_____

_____

_____

_____

WHAT DO YOU THINK? As you've seen, your beliefs about yourself, the world, and your future in it can either propel you forward or hold you back. Doubt and fear make it difficult and daunting to try anything, while confidence and gusto make you eager and excited about digging in. The same task can look like a mountain or a molehill, depending on the lens you look at it through. If you want to enjoy your journey, one of the best things you can do is train your mind to think about its challenges in a positive light. In this way, you can turn work into play.

WRITE NOW! What's something you're feeling hesitant about? Recast it in a positive light.

BECAUSE YOU COULD. The power of positive thinking has taken a lot of people a very long way throughout history. And maybe you've even experienced a bit of this yourself in your own life. Often when you're young, you don't know how hard something is, so you just do it. You spend a week hiking with no training; you join a band, even though you don't really know how to play an instrument; you create a series of paintings just because you feel like it. You have no self-doubts or fear about the undertaking, so you just chug right along doing something that, when you look back on it now, you can't believe you actually pulled off.

WRITE NOW! What's something impressive that you've accomplished simply because you didn't know it was supposed to be hard?

They can, because they think they can.

—Virgil

SWEET OF YOU TO SAY. There are no greater compliments than the ones we pay ourselves, but the ones other people give us are pretty great, too.

WRITE NOW! What's the best compliment you've ever received?

_____

_____

_____

_____

_____

PROGRESS, NOT PERFECTION. Reflect on your journal entries from the past week. Do you feel like you made progress? Do you feel like you enjoyed the journey and showed yourself love and care, or did you get hung up on perfection? Fill in the following progress bars to show how you feel about the week.

	1	5	10
Progress			
Enjoyment of the Journey			
Feelings of Self-Love			

WRITE NOW! What are your thoughts about this past week? Where did you make progress, and how did it feel?

_____

_____

OUCH. You were going along, doing your thing, making your progress when you hit a big pothole. You didn't anticipate some obstacle. You missed a deadline you set for yourself. You totally miscalculated what you needed to do. Whatever happened, you made a mistake and it *hurt*. But that's what happens. You make plans and then life comes in and laughs at them and kicks them over like a bully with a sandcastle. That's just part of the journey, and the trick of it is not letting it push you off your path entirely. The trick is to learn from it.

WRITE NOW! What painful mistake have you made on your journey? What have you learned from it?

I resolved to let no obstacle prevent me from putting forth the highest effort to fit myself to accomplish the most good in the world.

—Booker T. Washington

RIGHT TO BE WRONG. If you're on a journey to somewhere new, you're bound to get something wrong along the way. You have every right to be wrong. That's what gives you room to grow.

WRITE NOW! Do you feel you have a right to be wrong, or do you feel like you should get things right on the first try? Be honest!

_____

_____

_____

_____

_____

MY MISTAKE. Oftentimes, we are more forgiving when other people make mistakes than we are when the mistakes are our own.

WRITE NOW! How do you react to other people's mistakes? Are you easier on them than you are on yourself?

_____

_____

_____

_____

_____

BIG MISTAKE. If you're a human being, you've made a big mistake in your life. If you haven't, you should make sure you're not a robot. Because mistakes are as inevitable a part of being a person as love, heartbreak, laughter, and tears. We miscalculate and do the wrong thing. We get lazy and do the wrong thing. We get jealous or angry or shortsighted or a million other things and make a mistake that makes it feel that the sky is falling. But then the sky doesn't fall. You learn and go on living.

WRITE NOW! What is the biggest mistake you've ever made? What commensurately big lesson did you learn from that, and has it helped you on your journey?

FULL OF MISTAKES. If you're living big, going after big dreams, and taking risks, then your journey is going to be chock-full of mistakes. You don't know the future, so when you take a big risk to gain a big reward, sometimes it will pay off and sometimes it won't. That's the cost of a full life, of not always playing it safe. Instead of being put off by the idea that you've made mistakes and are inevitably going to make more of them, you can recognize them for what they are: proof that you're paying in enough to get something wonderful out of life. Big lessons, big rewards, big experiences.

WRITE NOW! What are some risks you can take that may end up being the kind of mistakes that make your journey fulfilling and enriching?

_Mistakes are part of the dues
one pays for a full life._

—Sophia Loren

REPEAT OFFENDER. Mistakes can be great when we learn from them. If you keep repeating the same ones, though, you need to think about how to get past them.

WRITE NOW! What's a mistake you've made more than once? How can you avoid doing it again?

_____

_____

_____

_____

_____

PROGRESS, NOT PERFECTION. Reflect on your journal entries from the past week. Do you feel like you made progress? Do you feel like you enjoyed the journey and showed yourself love and care, or did you get hung up on perfection? Fill in the following progress bars to show how you feel about the week.

	1	5	10
Progress			
Enjoyment of the Journey			
Feelings of Self-Love			

WRITE NOW! What are your thoughts about this past week? Where did you make progress, and how did it feel?

_____

_____

PROCRASTINATION HAPPENS. Putting off a difficult or unpleasant task is something everyone does—sometimes from time to time, sometimes all the time. It's a problem that builds on itself, because procrastinating feels bad in itself *and* you feel bad about doing it. Double whammy. One of the first things you need to do to get past procrastination is to forgive yourself for doing it in the past and know that it doesn't have to be your future. If you beat yourself up and believe you're just a lazy procrastinator, then you're almost certain to stay stuck. If you accept it as a fact of life that occasionally rears its head, you can get past it with self-love and ease.

WRITE NOW! Forgive yourself for having procrastinated in the past and reassure yourself that past procrastination doesn't define your future.

When we procrastinate, ... we know we are working against our own best interests.

—Piers Steel

NO MORE NONSENSE. Having a million things to do can keep you from doing anything at all. Take a look at your current to-do list. Is all of it *really* necessary?

WRITE NOW! What items can you strike from your to-do list because you don't have to do them?

CUE THE MUSIC. Having a cue that indicates *When this is done, I'm going to get to work* can be a powerful tool for beating procrastination. A bumping song works beautifully.

WRITE NOW! What song makes you want to jump up and get to work? Are there other cues you could use?

POWER HOUR. Giving a problem or a task an undivided hour of your attention can work miracles. This means getting rid of all distractions—no phones, no emails, no nothing. It's just you and the task at hand and whatever you need to wrestle it. Spend fifteen minutes doing your best to work on it, then take a five-minute break. Stretch, go for a short walk, whatever you like to do for a short rest. This doesn't mean spending five minutes doing a different task or talking to people. This is five minutes of quiet to let your mind kick the task around to see what shakes lose. Then go back to it for another fifteen minutes. Do this until the hour is up and you may just be amazed at how far you got.

WRITE NOW! Do a power hour and record how it went.

ARE YOUR REALLY PROCRASTINATING? You might put something off because you truly don't feel like doing it, or you might put something off because you're really not sure how to do it. Knowing the difference between those two things is critical. If you just don't feel like doing something, you can use this week's tricks to get started, and soon you'll feel great about finally putting the darn thing to rest. If you feel dread because you have to do something that feels overwhelming and nebulous, you're not procrastinating; you're just not prepared yet. The good news is, that's easy to deal with, too!

WRITE NOW! Break down a daunting task into small tasks you feel confident about.

Procrastination is the lazy cousin of fear. When we feel anxiety around an activity, we postpone it.

—Noelle Hancock, partially quoting her therapist

TAKE TIME TO REWARD YOURSELF. Another way to motivate yourself past procrastination is to promise yourself a reward once you take that step you have been avoiding.

WRITE NOW! What treat will you give yourself when you finally do that thing you've been putting off?

PROGRESS, NOT PERFECTION. Reflect on your journal entries from the past week. Do you feel like you made progress? Do you feel like you enjoyed the journey and showed yourself love and care, or did you get hung up on perfection? Fill in the following progress bars to show how you feel about the week.

	1	5	10
Progress			
Enjoyment of the Journey			
Feelings of Self-Love			

WRITE NOW! What are your thoughts about this past week? Where did you make progress, and how did it feel?

WHOLE AND COMPLETE. You can get so caught up trying to do something perfectly, the way you think it should be done, that you miss some really important stuff. If you look toward perfection or toward other people as the standards for what success looks like, you'll always miss the mark. You can't do it their way; you have to do it your way. If, instead, you spend time reflecting on what you want, what's important to you, what your goal looks like to you and no one else, then no matter where your journey takes you, you'll be able to find joy in knowing you're doing it your way for your own reasons. That's what makes you whole and complete.

WRITE NOW! How is pursuing your goal helping you to live authentically, to feel whole and complete?

The challenge is not to be perfect ... it's to be whole.

—Jane Fonda

IT'S ALIVE! Success isn't just a static achievement. You can be success in motion by living authentically and progressing toward your very own goals.

WRITE NOW! How are you already a great success?

_____

_____

_____

_____

_____

_____

A WINNER EVERY DAY! Each and every day that you make progress toward your goal is a day that you triumph.

WRITE NOW! What was your triumph today?

_____

_____

_____

_____

_____

_____

LOVE YOU MORE. This journey of yours started from a place of self-love, and after this long on the path, you've shown that love over and over again by showing up and working hard. You've likely also learned some things about yourself along the way. Strengths you didn't know you had, hang-ups you didn't think you could overcome but did, confidence in areas where you used to feel uncertain. The joy of the journey is not just the final attainment of the goal, but all these good things you gain along the way and the love you have for yourself that grows and grows.

WRITE NOW! What are some things you've grown to love about yourself on this journey?

BE YOUR OWN BEST FRIEND. If and when you find yourself feeling doubtful or self-critical for any reason, there is a simple exercise you can do to get yourself back on track and nip that negative self-talk right in the bud. All it takes is imagining that your best friend or close loved one is going through exactly what you're going through. You wouldn't berate them or scold them. You wouldn't call them names or tell them they're worthless. (Yet that's how we sometimes treat ourselves.) You'd tell them how much you love them and list all the things that make them amazing, and that's something you can do for yourself.

WRITE NOW! Compliment yourself the way you would your best friend if that person needed a pick-me-up.

We just need to be kinder to ourselves.
Truly, if we treated ourselves the way
we do our best friend, can you imagine
how much better off we would be?

—Meghan Markle

A GOOD DAY. Progress looks different from day to day, depending on where you are on your journey. But the feeling you get from a productive day is often the same.

WRITE NOW! How do you feel after a productive day?

_____

_____

_____

_____

_____

PROGRESS, NOT PERFECTION. Reflect on your journal entries from the past week. Do you feel like you made progress? Do you feel like you enjoyed the journey and showed yourself love and care, or did you get hung up on perfection? Fill in the following progress bars to show how you feel about the week.

	1	5	10
Progress			
Enjoyment of the Journey			
Feelings of Self-Love			

WRITE NOW! What are your thoughts about this past week? Where did you make progress, and how did it feel?

_____

_____

IT'S YOUR CUP, AFTER ALL. That old question about whether the cup is half full or half empty is meant to illustrate if you're an optimist or a pessimist. The truth is, you don't have to be either. The cup doesn't have to always be one way or the other, and neither do you. In all likelihood, the way you think about this age-old question depends on the day. And what's more, why not take control of the cup and decide when you need a little more or could do with a little less.

WRITE NOW! How are you feeling about the cup today?

The cup isn't half full or half empty, you're always topping it up.

—Rowena Cory Daniells

RUNNING LOW. Long weeks, too many appointments, dreary weather—we all have things that make us feel drained, and recognizing them can help you notice when you're going to need to recharge ahead of time.

WRITE NOW! What drains your cup?

FILL IT UP. When you're feeling like your cup is running a little low, it's important to take time to recharge.

WRITE NOW! What fills your cup?

GET OUT THERE. Studies have shown time and again that being in nature bolsters both your mental and physical health. Just taking a 40-second break to look at a picture of nature has been shown to improve not just focus but performance as well. Imagine what actually going outside can do for you then! The common wisdom for progress and productivity is to just keep your head down and power through, but the science increasingly shows that taking a green break is the best thing for you. So if you're feeling particularly drained, try a walk on the beach, a jaunt through the park, a hike in the woods, or a paddle down the river to refill your cup.

WRITE NOW! What is your favorite place to go in nature? How do you feel after a visit?

TABLE FOR ONE, PLEASE. Whether you think of yourself as an introvert or an extrovert, spending time alone is a necessary part of replenishing your energy reserves. It gives you time to appreciate yourself. You get to cultivate your own interests, be the center of your world, and enjoy the pleasure of your own company. If you're always in the company of others, no matter how awesome they are, you don't get the chance for reflection and rest that you need to keep going everyday—and to stay energized for your journey.

WRITE NOW! Plan a date with yourself to rest and recharge.

_Spending time alone in your own
company reinforces your self-worth
and is often the number-one way to
replenish your resilience reserves._

—Sam Owen

BREAK FOR FUN. It's tempting think that one day down the road, when all the work is done, you'll make time for more fun. The truth is, even when you reach your goal, there will always be work to do, so why not have some fun now?

WRITE NOW! What's your idea of fun?

_____

_____

_____

_____

PROGRESS, NOT PERFECTION. Reflect on your journal entries from the past week. Do you feel like you made progress? Do you feel like you enjoyed the journey and showed yourself love and care, or did you get hung up on perfection? Fill in the following progress bars to show how you feel about the week.

	1	5	10
Progress			
Enjoyment of the Journey			
Feelings of Self-Love			

WRITE NOW! What are your thoughts about this past week? Where did you make progress, and how did it feel?

_____

_____

KEEP YOUR BALANCE. Keeping up with the rest of your life while keeping up with your journey can be challenging. You have to strike a balance between the progress you want to continue making and everything else in your life that you love or have a responsibility for. If you're saying no to seeing friends and family time and again because you're working on your goal, you might be losing balance. Finding a rhythm to when you work and when you play will naturally help you achieve a balance between those two aspects of a happy life.

WRITE NOW! Do you feel like you have balance in your life? Is there anything you want to bring into better harmony?

Happiness is not a matter of intensity but of balance and order and rhythm and harmony.

—Thomas Merton

TOO MUCH. Keeping yourself in balance means recognizing when you're taking something too seriously or giving it too much of your attention.

WRITE NOW! Is there something on your journey you're giving too much weight to?

TOO LITTLE. Maintaining your balance also means noticing when you're not paying enough attention to something that deserves it.

WRITE NOW! Is there something on your journey you're not giving enough weight to?

NOTICE WHEN YOU NAIL IT. Part of fostering balance is recognizing when it happens. You may think that you'd feel a sense of balance if you just made more time for your friends, but then you notice that some of your friends demand too much of you and you feel better when you set boundaries. On the other hand, you may think that working harder on your goal will make you feel more balanced, but, in reality, taking breaks and going slow and steady better suit your natural rhythm.

WRITE NOW! When have you felt really balanced in your life? When you reflect on it, was there anything surprising or counterintuitive that was going on to help foster that balance?

BALANCING BELIEFS. Believing in yourself means believing in your decisions and your priorities. Because you have faith in yourself, you are less prone to questioning your choices and your actions. Instead, you can move forward with confidence, knowing that each step you take, even if it's the wrong one, is OK. You did your best and that is enough. You are enough. When you really accept this truth, the scales balance as a matter of course.

WRITE NOW! How are you feeling about your sense of self? Do you accept that you are enough?

Believing in our hearts that who we are is enough is the key to a more satisfying and balanced life.

—Ellen Sue Stern

THAT WORKS, TOO. Even if you're feeling off balance, there is a lesson to learn there. Taking note of what gives you the wobbles can help you restore your equilibrium.

WRITE NOW! What throws you off-balance? How can you change it?

_____   _____

_____

_____

_____

_____

PROGRESS, NOT PERFECTION. Reflect on your journal entries from the past week. Do you feel like you made progress? Do you feel like you enjoyed the journey and showed yourself love and care, or did you get hung up on perfection? Fill in the following progress bars to show how you feel about the week.

	1	5	10
Progress			
Enjoyment of the Journey			
Feelings of Self-Love			

WRITE NOW! What are your thoughts about this past week? Where did you make progress, and how did it feel?

_____

_____

WORSE THINGS THAN BEING TIRED. When you're tired, most times you should absolutely rest. But there are also times when you're tired but pushing through can help you to become reinvigorated or it can get you to the next level or to a goal that's more important to you than resting right this minute. There are, after all, worse things than being tired, such as letting yourself down or not being your best. It's up to you to look inside, see how you're feeling, and decide if now is a time when you should rest or a time when you should power through.

WRITE NOW! When have you pushed through despite being tired? Are you glad you did?

One may go a long way after one is tired.

—French proverb

GOOD MORNING. A great way to motivate yourself in the morning is to think about how you want to feel at the end of the day.

WRITE NOW! How do you want to feel when you go to bed tonight (or tomorrow night if you're writing late in the day)?

GOOD NIGHT. You can motivate yourself for tomorrow by thinking about what you want to accomplish, given that you've got a whole brand-new day to work with.

WRITE NOW! What do you want to accomplish tomorrow?

PUT IT TO REST. As you've seen by now, positive thinking goes a long way. Believing you can do something, really knowing it, helps you conquer even the biggest hurdle and carries you along to your goals with confidence and joy. A way to supercharge your positive mind-set is by affirming your intentions and goals before you go to sleep. As you're lying there, drifting off to the land of nod, visualize yourself taking the next step on your journey. Be sure to add in as many details as you can. Or if visualizations aren't your thing, you can repeat an emotionally powerful affirmation to yourself about how energized and capable you are. Either way, going to sleep with these reinforcing thoughts helps work them deep into your mind so they become second nature to you.

WRITE NOW! What will you imagine or repeat to yourself tonight before you go to sleep?

RIGHT NOW. When you're feeling overwhelmed by how much there is left to do on your journey—something every person striving for progress experiences—you can recapture your motivation and power by reminding yourself that, though the road is long, you only have to walk it one day at a time. While, of course, having a planned route is helpful, if you keep looking ahead you're likely to get dizzy and need to sit down. If you focus only on the path right in front of you, each step is much easier to take.

WRITE NOW! What is the step right in front of you?

No matter how difficult your situation is, you can get through it if you don't look too far into the future, and focus on the present moment. You can get through anything one day at a time.

—Bob Parsons

BIG AND SMALL. If you're here writing in this journal, it means you made progress today. Maybe you made a big stride or maybe you are just journaling. Both are progress.

WRITE NOW! What was your progress today?

_____

_____

_____

_____

_____

PROGRESS, NOT PERFECTION. Reflect on your journal entries from the past week. Do you feel like you made progress? Do you feel like you enjoyed the journey and showed yourself love and care, or did you get hung up on perfection? Fill in the following progress bars to show how you feel about the week.

	1	5	10
Progress			
Enjoyment of the Journey			
Feelings of Self-Love			

WRITE NOW! What are your thoughts about this past week? Where did you make progress, and how did it feel?

_____

_____

TAKE NOTE. By now you've had loads of accomplishments, big and small, on your journey of progress. Sometimes you celebrated them (hopefully!), but sometimes you didn't even notice them go by. This can happen when you're caught up in movement. The joy of the journey lies, in part, in being proud of yourself as you go along. You're doing hard work and that warrants recognition by yourself, at the very least. Every step is an accomplishment and deserves its own little happy dance. This will keep you feeling good about yourself and your progress, which is fuel for the trip.

WRITE NOW! List all the accomplishments you can think of from your journey so far.

Don't wait until you reach your goal to be proud of yourself. Be proud of every step you take.

—Karen Salmansohn

THE LITTLE ONE. Celebrating the small stuff, as you know, is a great motivator.

WRITE NOW! What's the tiniest accomplishment you can think of from your journey? Count it!

_____

_____

_____

_____

_____

THE BIG ONE. Remembering your biggest accomplishment(s) is proof of how utterly badass you are, which can lift you up when you're feeling down.

WRITE NOW! Pick a big accomplishment to be your progress mascot, one that you can look back on whenever you need a reminder of your baddassitude.

_____

_____

_____

_____

_____

_____

IT'S NOT ALL UPHILL. While making progress on your journey is often something that feels like you're hiking uphill, there are also times when you turn a corner and there's a smooth patch you can coast on. You've done a lot of hard work building up your strength and honing your skills, so now when you get down to business, sometimes it's almost effortless. While early on what you were doing was learning and planning, now you have the know-how and confidence to get steps done. The work feels easier, which is an accomplishment unto itself.

WRITE NOW! What skills and strengths have you acquired that have made the work easier?

TAKE IT ALL IN. When you still have a lot of road ahead of you, you can keep taking step after step without really noticing how far you've come. As we've learned this week, it's important to stop and take a look around you to marvel at all that beautiful progress you've made. To soak up the view and appreciate where you are at this very moment. You will never have this day again, so be sure to stop and honor it—to be proud of yourself for getting here.

WRITE NOW! Praise yourself for the progress you've made. Dwell on what you're proud of.

When you do something you are proud of, dwell on it a little, praise yourself for it, relish the experience, take it in.

—Mildred Newman and Bernard Berkowitz

GROWING, LEARNING. As you go along on this journey, you're likely learning lots of lessons about yourself.

WRITE NOW! What's the latest thing you've learned about you?

_____

_____

_____

_____

_____

PROGRESS, NOT PERFECTION. Reflect on your journal entries from the past week. Do you feel like you made progress? Do you feel like you enjoyed the journey and showed yourself love and care, or did you get hung up on perfection? Fill in the following progress bars to show how you feel about the week.

	1	5	10
Progress			
Enjoyment of the Journey			
Feelings of Self-Love			

WRITE NOW! What are your thoughts about this past week? Where did you make progress, and how did it feel?

_____

_____

GROUP WORK. On a journey of personal progress, it's tempting to try to do it all on your own. To feel that this is your path, so you must walk it alone. While it's true that you have to show up and do the work, it's also true that other people can help you along the way, and you can help them. Joining a group of people who are trying to reach goals similar to yours can keep you motivated, help hold you accountable, and inspire you. You can see how other people tackle problems and learn lessons from their triumphs—and mistakes!

WRITE NOW! What kind of group might you join to help you along? What do you think of this idea?

_____

_____

_____

_____

_____

_____

_____

_____

_____

*Find a group of people who challenge
and inspire you, spend a lot of time with
them, and it will change your life.*

—Amy Poehler

PERSONAL HERO. Having someone you admire, your own personal hero, is both heartening and inspiring.

WRITE NOW! What is one valuable lesson that you have learned from someone whom you admire?

POBODY'S NERFECT. While we can learn from other people's accomplishments, we can also learn from their mistakes.

WRITE NOW! What's one valuable lesson you've learned from someone else's mistake?

WORKOUT BUDDY. Whether or not you're into joining groups, having one person you can count on to keep you motivated and on task can be a great asset. A workout buddy, no matter what kind of work you're doing, is someone you can talk to about the challenges you're facing and someone who will understand what you're going through. They may have great advice, or they can act as a valuable sounding board. Plus, working on something in tandem means they're seeing your progress and that second set of eyes can do wonders for keeping you on track. And vice versa. It's a two-way street that will likely help both of you progress.

WRITE NOW! What qualities would you want in a workout buddy? Does anyone come to mind whom you could partner with?

FEEL THE SYNERGY. When you work with another person or in a group, you can create a synergy that helps everyone get to where they want to be. Each person has skills and knowledge and enthusiasm all their own, and when everyone pitches in what they have, the load is lighter for everyone. While you can accomplish so much on your own, you might be capable of even greater heights when you and your companions pool your strengths together.

WRITE NOW! Can you imagine being able to get farther in a group than on your own? Why or why not?

Alone we can do so little,
together we can do so much.

—Helen Keller

OFFER UP. At this point on your journey, you have a lot of expertise to share and you can find lots of people who'd like to hear what you have to say.

WRITE NOW! How do you feel about the idea of helping someone who is not as far along on their journey as you are?

PROGRESS, NOT PERFECTION. Reflect on your journal entries from the past week. Do you feel like you made progress? Do you feel like you enjoyed the journey and showed yourself love and care, or did you get hung up on perfection? Fill in the following progress bars to show how you feel about the week.

	1	5	10
Progress			
Enjoyment of the Journey			
Feelings of Self-Love			

WRITE NOW! What are your thoughts about this past week? Where did you make progress, and how did it feel?

WHEN YOU'RE STUCK. Boy, oh boy, have you been working hard! Good for you! Hopefully you're taking time to appreciate all you've accomplished. But even with all your strides, there's still that one area you're stuck in; some step you haven't yet managed to work through, even though you've been trying. Oftentimes, when we're stuck on something, that means there's a lesson we still have to learn. You might need a new approach or have to take a risk or do something that makes you uncomfortable. The lesson is always different, but by taking an honest look at the problem, you can always figure it out.

WRITE NOW! What's something you've been stuck on? How can you adjust your approach to finally figure it out?

Nothing ever goes away until it has taught us what we need to know.

—Pema Chödrön

Date

Date

Week 36 * Day 2

WHAT RUT? If you're feeling stuck in a progress rut, you might need to let go of something that's holding you back.

WRITE NOW! Do you have any entrenched habits or timeworn stories you tell yourself that could be the reason you're feeling held back?

Date

Week 36 * Day 3

LOOK AT IT THIS WAY. Changing the way you look at a problem, or even your progress, might be just what you need to jump to the next step.

WRITE NOW! What's something you'd like to change your perspective on?

CHANGE UP. There is no journey that doesn't have its plateaus. Times when you're working hard, you're doing all the things that have propelled you forward in the past, and you're keeping at it each and every day, but yet you don't seem to be going forward. You're on a treadmill instead of a path. If you want to get off a plateau, you often have to shake things up. Maybe you need to do some research, reach out to friends or experts, or reup your efforts. After all, doing the same things over and over again is not how you change results.

WRITE NOW! What's a big change you might need to make to get off a plateau?

WALK IT OFF. The benefits of walking can be felt in the body, mind, and soul. If you're stuck on a problem, walking can shake the answer loose from your brain. It might be the enchanting rhythm of step after step, the change of scenery, the freedom you give yourself when you decide to go for a walk for the sake of just taking a break. Whatever the magic is, and it's likely different magic for everyone, there's no denying that, when all else fails, stretching your legs in the fresh air can do wonders.

WRITE NOW! Take a good long walk, then record how you feel.

*Every day I walk myself into a state
of well-being and walk away from every illness;
I have walked myself into my best thoughts,
and I know of no thought so burdensome
that one cannot walk away from it.*

—Søren Kierkegaard

IF ALL ELSE FAILS. If you're still feeling stuck after this week, try putting into words what you want next—your precise next step or mini goal. Clarity can spring loose the idea you need.

WRITE NOW! What exactly do you want next?

_____

_____

_____

_____

_____

PROGRESS, NOT PERFECTION. Reflect on your journal entries from the past week. Do you feel like you made progress? Do you feel that you've enjoyed the journey and showed yourself love and care, or did you get hung up on perfection? Fill in the following progress bars to show how you feel about the week.

	1	5	10
Progress			
Enjoyment of the Journey			
Feelings of Self-Love			

WRITE NOW! What are your thoughts about this past week? Where did you make progress, and how did it feel?

_____

_____

WHAT IT IS TO THRIVE. Thriving is about being at your best—doing what you most want to do, what you love to do, and nailing it. It can come after you achieve a big goal and are living with the benefits of that success, but it can also come well before that. You're thriving once you've hit your stride on a journey and are filled with the joy and energy of making beautiful progress. In a way, it's the peak of what it means to enjoy the journey. You're living your purpose and that fills each day with immediate meaning and future possibility.

WRITE NOW! In what ways do you feel like you're thriving on your journey?

_We thrive not when we've done it all,
but when we still have more to do._

—Sarah Lewis

NOTHING IS PERFECT. Thriving doesn't mean perfection in all areas of your life or your journey. You can be thriving in some things and still have other areas you want to improve on.

WRITE NOW! Do you feel like there are some obstacles keeping your from thriving in certain areas?

_____

_____

_____

_____

_____

YOUR MOVE. As with all parts of the journey, having a plan—and acting on it—is all you need to make progress, even when the going is tough.

WRITE NOW! How do you plan to overcome the obstacles keeping you from thriving?

_____

_____

_____

_____

_____

LEARNING BY EXAMPLE. One of the best, most effective ways to learn is by the example of others. Whether it's a famous person you've never met, a loved one, or a member of your community whom you admire, taking a page from the book of someone you see as thriving can help inspire you to do the same. Maybe they seem indefatigable to you, or endlessly kind and generous, or openhearted and open-minded in a way that's exceedingly hard to be in our modern world. And while there is so much to learn by paying close attention to their example, the thing that really drives the lesson home is direct experience; that is, trying it out for yourself.

WRITE NOW! Who is someone you see as thriving? What are their most admirable qualities, and how can you try to hone them in yourself?

IT'S ABOUT PERCEPTION. When you're truly thriving, you gain the uncanny ability not just to weather the storm but to dance in the rain. Challenges begin to morph into opportunities to grow stronger and get better. Setbacks offer lessons you're excited to learn. Instead of dreading the twists and turns of the journey, or being fearful of what's around the next corner and whether you'll be able to handle it, you feel confident in your ability to navigate around them and even a little eager to try your hand at the course.

WRITE NOW! How do you feel about the twists and turns you see ahead? Are you able to see some of them as opportunities or adventures?

It's better to be brave and dance in the rain, than to be scared hiding in the dark.

—Kyle Jessen

GIVING THANKS. One thing you can do to help yourself thrive is to practice gratitude. Meditating on what you're thankful for reminds you that, in many ways, you're already thriving.

WRITE NOW! What are you most grateful for this week?

_____

_____

_____

_____

_____

PROGRESS, NOT PERFECTION. Reflect on your journal entries from the past week. Do you feel like you made progress? Do you feel like you enjoyed the journey and showed yourself love and care, or did you get hung up on perfection? Fill in the following progress bars to show how you feel about the week.

	1	5	10
Progress			
Enjoyment of the Journey			
Feelings of Self-Love			

WRITE NOW! What are your thoughts about this past week? Where did you make progress, and how did it feel?

_____

_____

ENJOY IT. You've taken so many steps on your journey, and whether they were easy or difficult, hard-won or taken with aplomb, hopefully you enjoyed them. And that might mean they were fun, which is what we most often think of when we say we enjoyed something, but it could also mean they boosted your confidence, upped your strength, or taught you something in your misstep. To enjoy the journey doesn't just mean having a smile on your face as you skip through the daisies. It means you were there, in the moment, taking in and appreciating each step for what it was, and letting that build you up instead of tear you down.

WRITE NOW! In that spirit, how have you enjoyed your journey so far?

Aim for the sky, but move slowly, enjoying every step along the way. It is all those little steps that make the journey complete.

—Chanda Kochhar

DISTRACTIONS. *Enjoy the journey* is another way of saying *Be mindful of the present moment*. This is not always easy when you're working toward a goal.

WRITE NOW! What distracts you from being present?

_____

_____

_____

_____

_____

TUNE IN TO THIS TIME. Bringing your mind to the current moment is something that gets easier and easier the more you do it, which makes a journey better and better.

WRITE NOW! What helps you tune in to the current moment? Keep this in mind the next time you notice that you're distracted by the past or the future.

_____

_____

_____

_____

_____

SELF-COMPASSION. It's not easy to "enjoy" a difficult step on a journey. Setbacks and obstacles that threaten to derail and demoralize you are par for the course when you set a big goal in your life. As you know well by now, learning from these and keeping on the path anyway is what gets each and every successful person to their goal. Another strategy for dealing with hard moments and turning them into something you can feel good about is practicing self-compassion. If you're tired or made a mistake or took a misstep, by being compassionate with yourself—say, the way you would treat a loved one who did the same thing—you can find the value in even the hardest trial, and therein lies the joy of the journey.

WRITE NOW! Could you respond to difficulties that you encounter with more self-compassion? How?

WHAT MATTERS. When you're going after a big goal, even if you do practice mindfulness, you still likely have one eye on the prize. The goal is what keeps you motivated when things get tough, and it's your whole reason for embarking on the journey. That kind of determination is certainly not a bad thing! But it's the work, the journey, the endeavoring that cure the discontent, restlessness, or lack that put you on the path in the first place. So while getting to your goal will be extraordinary, in many of the ways that really matter, you've already succeeded.

WRITE NOW! How do you feel about yourself now in comparison to when you started your journey?

It's not the end result that matters,
it's the endeavoring that's the cure.

—Alisson Furman

USE YOUR SENSES. When you're feeling distracted and want to root yourself in the current moment, you can try this sensory exercise.

WRITE NOW! List five things you see, four things you hear, three things you feel, two things you smell, and one thing you taste.

_____

_____

_____

_____

_____

PROGRESS, NOT PERFECTION. Reflect on your journal entries from the past week. Do you feel like you made progress? Do you feel like you enjoyed the journey and showed yourself love and care, or did you get hung up on perfection? Fill in the following progress bars to show how you feel about the week.

	1	5	10
Progress			
Enjoyment of the Journey			
Feelings of Self-Love			

WRITE NOW! What are your thoughts about this past week? Where did you make progress, and how did it feel?

_____

_____

YOU'RE NEARLY THERE! Well done! You've made it to the three-quarter mark, and that really is something to celebrate. This is a great opportunity to take a look around you and see how you're making your dream into reality. You've used and built so much strength to get you this far, and there is still so much wonder that is yet to come. Now that your goal is coming closer and closer, the details of it are probably coming into clearer focus.

WRITE NOW! What details of your dream have come into view now that it's becoming more and more real?

_____

_____

_____

_____

_____

_____

_____

*There are some people who live
in a dream world, and there are some
who face reality; and then there are
those who turn one into the other.*

—attributed to Douglas H. Everett

REST STOP. When the road is long, it's tempting to stop at a pretty point along the way and just stay there.

WRITE NOW! When have you felt like stopping?

_____

_____

_____

_____

_____

_____

GET GOING. Rest stops are just stops where you rest. Not where you stay, as you well know, you intrepid journeyer.

WRITE NOW! What gets you going again?

_____

_____

_____

_____

_____

_____

DO YOU NEED THAT? After this long on the road, it's a good idea to take a look in your pack and see if there's anything you can unload. You might have old ideas or ideals that you don't need anymore, that might even be getting in the way of your progress. You might have picked up an exercise or practice along the way that served you well getting you up one hill, but now you no longer need it. Just because you've hit your stride doesn't mean you should take for granted that you know the best way to do things. An open mind and a critical eye can always help you make progress.

WRITE NOW! Is there anything you've picked up along the way that you might not need anymore?

IGNORE THE SIRENS. There is a funny thing that can happen when you get this close to a goal. You may begin to flag. You might ease up from the gas and maybe begin to rest on your laurels a bit, to mix some metaphors. Maybe you start to take breaks even when you don't need them. And getting started again becomes harder and harder. There is a siren song luring you to slow down, and, before you know it, you've stopped on their island for far too long. Before this siren song can tempt you, recommit.

WRITE NOW! Revisit the glory that is your goal and recommit to getting there.

_____

_____

_____

_____

_____

_____

_____

_____

Some ... abandon their purposes when close to the goal; while it is at that particular point, more than at any other, that others secure the victory over their rivals.

—Polybius

LOVE THAT PROGRESS. Take a look back over the past few months to see all that you've accomplished.

WRITE NOW! What are you most proud of from the last three months?

➡

_____

_____

_____

_____

_____

PROGRESS, NOT PERFECTION. Reflect on your journal entries from the past week. Do you feel like you made progress? Do you feel like you enjoyed the journey and showed yourself love and care, or did you get hung up on perfection? Fill in the following progress bars to show how you feel about the week.

	1	5	10
Progress			
Enjoyment of the Journey			
Feelings of Self-Love			

WRITE NOW! What are your thoughts about this past week? Where did you make progress, and how did it feel?

➡

_____

_____

YOU KNOW THE WAY. At no point on your journey are you alone. While there are those who inspire you, encourage you, and give you strength, there are also those who would get in the way of your progress. They likely don't mean any harm, but some people are in the slow lane and would slow you down with them. There are also people who think they know the road better than you and are really pushy about convincing you to do things their way. People who just don't think you should be on the road at all—it's not safe. Everyone is eager to give directions, but only you know where you're going. You just have to trust yourself.

WRITE NOW! When have you listened to your gut and were absolutely right?

_____

_____

_____

_____

_____

_____

_____

_____

This life is mine alone. So I have stopped asking people for directions to places they've never been. There is no map. We are all pioneers.

—Glennon Doyle

GO WITH YOUR GUT. Sometimes you just *know* when something is right or wrong, and the more you tune in to what that feeling is like, the more it will speak to you.

WRITE NOW! Describe that gut feeling as best you can.

_____

_____

_____

_____

_____

TAP IN. Intuition happens when you take the time to look inward to see how you're feeling below the surface.

WRITE NOW! What is my intuition saying about this moment on my journey?

_____

_____

_____

_____

_____

_____

ASK IT. As you hone your intuition, it becomes more and more available to you. Instead of just being struck by a gut instinct from time to time, you can look inward and ask your intuition to guide you on something specific. This can help you solve a problem, decide on a next step, get off a plateau, or help you move past whatever the obstacle is at the moment. It can even just let you know that all is well and that you're on the right path. Asking yourself what you want and what you need is a way to tap into your intuition about your next steps.

WRITE NOW! Ask yourself what you want and what you need next.

WITHOUT A DOUBT. Clearing out self-doubt is the final step in being able to clearly hear what your intuition is telling you. The noise of self-doubt—that voice that questions and criticizes and jeers and just churns out negativity—can grow so loud that you can't hear the truth that your spirit is whispering to you. That you can, that you know how, that you will, that you already are. Those truths are scary because it seems like you need to risk disappointment and failure to live them, but by just trying to live them, you've already succeeded.

WRITE NOW! What lingering self-doubts do you have? Write them down, then cross them right the hell out. Write about why they're untrue.

You will never follow your own inner voice until you clear up the doubts in your mind.

—Roy T. Bennett

JUST LISTEN. This week you've made a lot of progress listening to your intuition and trusting yourself to know your own path.

WRITE NOW! Close your eyes and think about your path. What does your intuition say about it?

_____

_____

_____

_____

_____

PROGRESS, NOT PERFECTION. Reflect on your journal entries from the past week. Do you feel like you made progress? Do you feel like you enjoyed the journey and showed yourself love and care, or did you get hung up on perfection? Fill in the following progress bars to show how you feel about the week.

	1	5	10
Progress			
Enjoyment of the Journey			
Feelings of Self-Love			

WRITE NOW! What are your thoughts about this past week? Where did you make progress, and how did it feel?

_____

_____

TWISTS AND TURNS. A journey is not always a straightforward path. There is not one main highway to take, with clear signs pointing you where you need to go next, telling you where to turn and when to rest. You must map or blaze the trail yourself, and sometimes, you may get lost. When you don't know where to turn, or you went the wrong way, you have to figure out how to get back on the path you want. At that point, turn inward to find your strength and regain your footing. If you listen closely, your intuition will point you where to go next.

WRITE NOW! Close your eyes and meditate on who you are right now, despite any muddy water obscuring your path. Focus on your strengths and beauty, and record them here.

_____

_____

_____

_____

_____

*If you feel lost, disappointed, hesitant,
or weak, return to yourself, to who
you are, here and now and when you get
there, you will discover yourself, like
a lotus flower in full bloom, even in a
muddy pond, beautiful and strong.*

—Masaru Emoto

FORK IN THE ROAD. If you're feeling lost or trying to choose a way to go, try listing all the potential paths you could take forward

WRITE NOW! What are the next steps you could take?

_____

_____

_____

_____

_____

_____

PICTURE EACH PATH. One by one, imagine that you've taken each of the steps from yesterday.

WRITE NOW! What is your reaction? How do you feel when you picture each one?

_____

_____

_____

_____

_____

GETTING OUT OF THE WEEDS. When you're deep into a journey, sometimes you get lost in the weeds. Being uncertain about the details of what to do next can bog you down and obscure the path. When you can't quite see which way to go, reminding yourself of your values, the reason you're going after your goal in the first place, can make the path appear in front of you. Going back to the core like that, the why of the whole endeavor, can clear away the brush so you can start moving forward again, instead of remaining snagged on the thorns along the way.

WRITE NOW! What are the core values that inspired this journey in the first place?

NOT ACTUALLY LOST. When you feel like you've taken a wrong turn, you may panic or lose heart. But when this happens, it's actually an opportunity to look around and see where you truly are. A wrong turn can take you where you didn't know you wanted to be, but if you don't stop to look around and honestly ask yourself how you feel, you might keep charging toward what you thought you wanted without realizing that you've gotten somewhere even better. This sort of change can be painful and difficult to recognize, but it's the sort of transformation you don't want to miss.

WRITE NOW! Take a hard look at where you're going. Is there a greater dream than the one you planned unfolding before you?

It takes tremendous strength to let go of what you thought your life should be and surrender yourself to the greater unfolding of what life's dream is for you.

—Nicky Clinch

GO BACK. Getting back on track can be as easy as going back to your original plan, pinpointing where you are, and letting that reveal your next steps.

WRITE NOW! According to your original plan, what should your next step be?

_____

_____

_____

_____

_____

PROGRESS, NOT PERFECTION. Reflect on your journal entries from the past week. Do you feel like you made progress? Do you feel like you enjoyed the journey and showed yourself love and care, or did you get hung up on perfection? Fill in the following progress bars to show how you feel about the week.

	1	5	10
Progress			
Enjoyment of the Journey			
Feelings of Self-Love			

WRITE NOW! What are your thoughts about this past week? Where did you make progress, and how did it feel?

_____

_____

FEELING GOOD. The time you've spent on this journey is a remarkable feat in and of itself, and it's likely that you've done a lot of remarkable things along the way. After all, working toward your goal over this past year has taken loads of planning and course corrections, determination, perseverance, grit, and so much more. By now, you've probably acquired and honed skills you didn't even know you'd gain. No matter what your goal is, the journey has been one of self-improvement, and that's gotta feel good!

WRITE NOW! How has your progress made you feel? How has it affected your confidence?

The key to happiness is really progress and growth and constantly working on yourself and developing something. It's when we stop growing [that] things start to get frustrating.

—Lewis Howes

INCREMENTAL IMPROVEMENT. You've been undergoing a lot of incremental improvements on this journey, and it can be heartening to look back and reflect on how far you've come.

WRITE NOW! List the improvements you've seen in yourself over the course of your journey.

_____

_____

_____

_____

_____

PICKING FAVORITES. While you should be proud of all the improvements you've made so far, there is probably one that really stands out.

WRITE NOW! Which improvement are you most proud of and why?

_____

_____

_____

_____

_____

_____

GOOD DAY. Each day you work toward your goal is a good day. This doesn't mean that you can see results every day from your close-up perspective, nor does it mean that you're always improving at a steady pace. The journey is often traveled in fits and starts. You make giant strides forward and then plateau for a while. The uneven road can be a difficult one, but you can make it a little smoother by thinking about the things that you are doing well right at this moment. Focusing on the here and now and counting all the things you did well today will make feeling prepared for tomorrow that much easier.

WRITE NOW! What are all the things you did really well today?

WALKING THE LINE. Improvement happens when you meet a challenge. If something is easy to do, you've already mastered the skill, which is an awesome place to be, but being good is not the same thing as getting better. If you want to keep improving, you need challenges. But they have to be challenges you're ready to meet. So not too easy, not too hard. This balance is something you probably learned firsthand on this journey, and reflecting on it can help you maintain balance throughout the rest of your journey and beyond.

WRITE NOW! What challenge have you met that felt really good and kept you motivated? What do you think your next one should be?

_____

_____

_____

_____

_____

_____

_____

Improvement requires a delicate balance. You need to regularly search for challenges that push you to your edge while continuing to make enough progress to stay motivated.

—James Clear

WHAT'S LEFT. After reflecting this week on all the improvements you've made so far, it's time to look at the other side of the coin to see what's left to improve on.

WRITE NOW! What is one thing you want to be sure you improve on by the end of this journal?

_____

_____

_____

_____

PROGRESS, NOT PERFECTION. Reflect on your journal entries from the past week. Do you feel like you made progress? Do you feel like you enjoyed the journey and showed yourself love and care, or did you get hung up on perfection? Fill in the following progress bars to show how you feel about the week.

	1	5	10
Progress			
Enjoyment of the Journey			
Feelings of Self-Love			

WRITE NOW! What are your thoughts about this past week? Where did you make progress, and how did it feel?

_____

_____

NOW AND THEN. As you've gone along on this journey, you've likely noticed that there are a few things you need to keep in balance. We've explored work and rest as well as challenges and success. There is also a balance to be found between planning ahead and being in the moment. You need to plot your course, but also recognize when it needs correcting. The joy is in the moments of the journey, yet the journey requires planning. When you're driven toward a goal, it's easy to get lost in the mapping and neglect the mindfulness, but then you can miss out on the soul of the trip. Appreciating the here and now is what gives joy to the journey.

WRITE NOW! The really great things that are happening right now are . . .

It makes no difference how many peaks you reach if there was no pleasure in the climb.

—Oprah Winfrey

BONUS! For all your careful planning, odds are that your journey has yielded something unexpected and beneficial.

WRITE NOW! What's an unexpected, positive thing that's come from your journey? Be as specific as you can.

YOU NEED YOU. Taking care of yourself never gets old or irrelevant. Check in with yourself to make sure you're meeting all your self-care needs.

WRITE NOW! What are your next three acts of self-care going to be?

FLIP THE SCRIPT. We learn through our mistakes and failures even more than through our triumphs and successes—something you've likely experienced yourself by now on your journey. When something doesn't work or hurts or you get some other negative outcome, you figure out a better way to go. The problem is, even when you've learned the lesson, the pain of the past mistake or failure may linger. Your mind is so hardwired to learn from negative experiences that it may fixate on the hurt even when it's OK to move on. Getting past these mental snags takes conscious effort. You need to write your own script, so your brain knows it's all right to let it go.

WRITE NOW! Think of something from your journey that you've learned from, but still don't feel great about. Write about how positively things turned out and tell yourself you're letting it go.

TAKE STOCK. As you've learned, going forward requires you to look around from time to time to see how you're doing and make sure the way you're going is the best path for you. It's also good to check if you've got any pebbles in your shoe. Meaning: Is there something that's been nagging at you on this journey? A concern or problem you've pushed down because you could keep going despite it? (Also see week 9, day 1.) Now's a good time to shake that pebble free so it doesn't ultimately do anything that holds you back.

WRITE NOW! Is there a pebble in your shoe that you need to deal with? How will you handle it?

The reality we ignore or deny is the one that weakens our most impassioned efforts toward improvement.

—Katherine Dunn

OLD HABITS DIE HARD. Even after all this time making progress, you might still be trying to get something perfect. There's no shame in that! It's hard to give up on that particular myth.

WRITE NOW! Is there anything you're still trying to perfect, instead of make progress on?

PROGRESS, NOT PERFECTION. Reflect on your journal entries from the past week. Do you feel like you made progress? Do you feel like you enjoyed the journey and showed yourself love and care, or did you get hung up on perfection? Fill in the following progress bars to show how you feel about the week.

	1	5	10
Progress			
Enjoyment of the Journey			
Feelings of Self-Love			

WRITE NOW! What are your thoughts about this past week? Where did you make progress, and how did it feel?

REPEAT YOURSELF. A big part of getting all the way to your goal is having the tenacity and stamina to repeat yourself. To practice and improve. To fail and learn. To keep going, practicing the same skills over and over again until you get as near to perfect as is humanly possible. This ability to do something over and over again—and still love doing it, still learn from it, still improve upon it and keep growing so it stays interesting—is a key element in making dreams into something real. It's the work that allows you to find success.

WRITE NOW! How has your practice changed since you started on your journey?

_____

_____

_____

_____

_____

_____

_____

_____

Success itself is a habit. . . . Successful people do things a certain way. They do these things over and over again.

—Dwayne Thomas

GETTING CLOSE. They say practice makes perfect, and while we know that's not true—perfect is impossible—it does get you as close as you can get.

WRITE NOW! How has the way you practice improved since the start of your journey?

_____

_____

_____

_____

_____

GETTING MOVING. You know you should practice often or even every day, but sometimes that can be hard to do.

WRITE NOW! What motivates you to practice when you're not feeling it?

_____

_____

_____

_____

_____

_____

LEVEL UP. Practice involves repeating the same things over and over again to improve on key skills, some of which can feel tedious even when you're doing something you love. But it's also exciting when you finally nail what you've been working to do. You improve slowly, day by day, and then Bam! You're doing something that once seemed so hard it was nearly impossible. The work is the only way you're going to get to your goal, but that doesn't mean you should be continually bored by it. When you're losing interest in your daily practice, that just means it's time to take it to the next level.

WRITE NOW! What could help you take your practice to the next level?

PRACTICE PAYS. Sure, practicing something every day can have its moments of, let's say, tedium, but it also pays off in so many ways and can even become a joy in itself. It can straddle that double goodness of moving you along your path toward your goal and being a pleasure in the present. Once you're good at something, once you've mastered it, practicing it can feel great. It can bring you into the flow state, it can help you blow off steam, it can make you feel like you're living your purpose. All this while moving you ever closer toward your goal.

WRITE NOW! What do you love about practicing? How does it make you feel? Have your feelings toward it changed over your journey?

_____

_____

_____

_____

_____

_____

_____

_____

_____

Once you learn something,
it feels good to practice it.

—Barbara Oakley

A PRACTICAL FRIEND. If you're having trouble practicing as often as you like, find a friend who's also on a journey and hold each other accountable.

WRITE NOW! Who can be your practice pal? What schedule would you like to keep?

_____

_____

_____

_____

_____

PROGRESS, NOT PERFECTION. Reflect on your journal entries from the past week. Do you feel like you made progress? Do you feel like you enjoyed the journey and showed yourself love and care, or did you get hung up on perfection? Fill in the following progress bars to show how you feel about the week.

	1	5	10
Progress			
Enjoyment of the Journey			
Feelings of Self-Love			

WRITE NOW! What are your thoughts about this past week? Where did you make progress, and how did it feel?

_____

_____

SAME OBSTACLES, NEW YOU. Without a doubt, you've grown and learned along the course of your journey. The ways in which you respond to challenges and obstacles have probably changed along with you. Some walls that would have seemed insurmountable in the past may now be totally scalable. You may even be excited to face them, eager to see what you can learn from facing them and getting past them.

WRITE NOW! As you look back over the course of your journey so far, how has the way you see and respond to obstacles changed?

_____

_____

_____

_____

_____

_____

_____

_____

Obstacles don't have to stop you.
If you run into a wall, don't turn around
and give up. Figure out how to climb it,
go through it, or work around it.

—Michael Jordan

SETBACKS. You've likely faced your share of setbacks over the course of this journey, and as you've progressed down your path, the way you feel about those moments has probably changed.

WRITE NOW! Looking back, how do you feel now about the setbacks you faced?

_____

_____

_____

_____

_____

LEAPS FORWARD. For any setbacks you've faced, you probably had some great wins to balance them out and keep you going.

WRITE NOW! Looking back, how do you feel about the wins you've had?

THE QUALITY THAT COUNTS. If you're still here, writing in this journal, you've had tenacity for days. And months. Literally. As you've proceeded on this journey, both in this journal and firsthand, you've recognized that determination—more than talent or genius or anything else—is what gets you to your goal. Coming back day after day, taking step after step, is the only thing that carries you to the finish line. You've proven you've got what it takes to chase your dreams, and that's a rare thing. Hopefully, you're celebrating yourself quite a bit these days. When you started, though, you might not have known that you would make it this far.

WRITE NOW! How did you feel about your likelihood of success when you started? How has that feeling changed over the course of the journey so far?

THE OPINION THAT COUNTS. The farther you get on a personal journey, the stronger your confidence can become. When you prove to yourself time and again that you're capable of doing more than you thought, and you've got the drive to do the real work it takes to live your dream, your confidence skyrockets—and rightly so. As your confidence grows, often the opinions and criticisms of others get quieter and quieter. You know your own capabilities much better than anyone else, so no matter what someone else believes about you, you know that what you believe about yourself is the only opinion that really counts.

WRITE NOW! How has the weight you give to other people's opinions changed over the course of your journey?

It took me a long time not to judge myself through someone else's eyes.

—Sally Field

GROWTH AND CHANGE. This week you took a look at the amazing growth and change you've made so far, but the journey isn't over yet.

WRITE NOW! How else would you like to grow on the rest of your journey?

PROGRESS, NOT PERFECTION. Reflect on your journal entries from the past week. Do you feel like you made progress? Do you feel like you enjoyed the journey and showed yourself love and care, or did you get hung up on perfection? Fill in the following progress bars to show how you feel about the week.

	1	5	10
Progress			
Enjoyment of the Journey			
Feelings of Self-Love			

WRITE NOW! What are your thoughts about this past week? Where did you make progress, and how did it feel?

FACE IT. To grow and get stronger and get closer to your goal, you have to face a whole host of fears. Some are common to all journeys—fear of failure, fear that you're not good enough, fear that you've made a wrong choice—and some are specific to you and your goal. These are not easy things. But each time you face down a fear, your bravery grows. You become that much more confident that the next time something comes along that scares you, you'll be able to deal with it.

WRITE NOW! How do you respond to fear now in contrast to how you responded to it at the start of your journey?

You gain strength, courage and confidence by every experience in which you really stop to look fear in the face. . . . You must do the thing you think you cannot do.

—Eleanor Roosevelt

THAT THING. When you first started out and had the whole road ahead of you, you probably had one fear in particular that scared the pants off you.

WRITE NOW! What scared you at the start of this journey?

➡️

_____

_____

_____

_____

_____

_____

YOU CAN'T AVOID IT. To get to your goal, facing that big fear is unavoidable. By now you've probably had to face it in some way.

WRITE NOW! How did you slay that fear or, if you're still dealing with it, what's your plan to vanquish it?

➡️

_____

_____

_____

_____

_____

SAY ITS NAME. Sometimes fear isn't something specific. Sometimes it's more of a vague dread. There's something unsettling lurking and you don't know exactly what it is. Maybe it's the deep-down fear that no matter what you do, you won't actually get to your goal. Maybe it's uncertainty itself—not knowing exactly what your next steps are or how things are going to turn out. If you want to fight your fears, you have to face them, and to face them, it helps to know exactly what they are. Having a foggy sense of uncertainty prohibits you from being able to burn off the mist. Knowing what's truly out there means you can plan to vanquish it.

WRITE NOW! What vague fear do you have? Can you name it?

NOT EASY, BUT SO WORTH IT. Progress is no easy feat. It is something you have to choose to strive for day after day. You have to recommit to your goal and face your fears over and over again, both old ones and new ones. If you're still here, though, you've found the strength to make these tough choices again and again, and that commitment makes you amazing. It shows that you're living with purpose, and that in itself makes for a life well lived.

WRITE NOW! What gives you the strength to face your fears again and again?

_____

_____

_____

_____

_____

_____

_____

Growth [is] seen as an endless series of daily choices and decisions in each of which one can choose to go back toward safety or forward toward growth. Growth must be chosen again and again; fear must be overcome again and again.

—Abraham Maslow

NEXT! You've faced down countless fears by now, but the journey isn't over yet. There's likely still a troll to grapple with under the next bridge

WRITE NOW! What is something you're still afraid of, a fear you still want to overcome?

_____

_____

_____

_____

_____

PROGRESS, NOT PERFECTION. Reflect on your journal entries from the past week. Do you feel like you made progress? Do you feel like you enjoyed the journey and showed yourself love and care, or did you get hung up on perfection? Fill in the following progress bars to show how you feel about the week.

	1	5	10
Progress			
Enjoyment of the Journey			
Feelings of Self-Love			

WRITE NOW! What are your thoughts about this past week? Where did you make progress, and how did it feel?

_____

_____

READY FOR IT. Life lessons are a dime a dozen if you go online, watch TV, or read magazines and books. There is no end to the tales of hard-won wisdom that the teller wants you to take to heart. Work hard, keep at it, believe in yourself, take risks. These lessons are everywhere (including in this journal), but you can't really appreciate them until you're ready. You can only recognize the truth of these somewhat clichéd lessons if you've lived through something that taught them to you or prepared you for them in some way. Otherwise, you're just nodding along, knowing a particular lesson might be true but not *feeling* it.

WRITE NOW! What's a clichéd life lesson have you learned on your journey?

Life is a succession of lessons which must be lived to be understood.

—Ralph Waldo Emerson

Date   Week 47 * Day 2

YOU'RE HERE! Getting to week 47 is nothing to sneeze at. Obviously, you've learned a thing or two about how to persevere or you wouldn't be here.

WRITE NOW! What have you learned about your ability to persevere on your journey?

Date   Week 47 * Day 3

YOU'RE GREAT! No matter how you slice it, you need to believe in yourself pretty darn hard to show up for yourself for this long.

WRITE NOW! What have you learned about self-confidence on your journey?

WE WORK FOR YOU. This journal has been full of advice for how to keep going on a long journey of progress, and you've probably encountered a lot of advice reaching your goals outside this book as well. Hopefully, some of it resonated with you, but, more than likely, not all of it did. As important as it is to learn what works for you, it's just as important to learn what doesn't work for you. Detailed planning, affirmations, joining support groups, and all the rest—they work for some people and not for others. As long as you know what works for you, you'll be unstoppable.

WRITE NOW! What doesn't work for you?

YOU'RE THE BOSS. By this point on your journey, maybe you've seen that you are in charge of you and your destiny. You have the hand you are dealt, for sure, but you decide what to do with the cards. Your thoughts and actions really do create what happens in your life. As you come to appreciate this, to see how free you are, you'll also notice that the choices you make show you a lot about yourself. The journey you choose and the actions you take on while on your path tell the story of you.

WRITE NOW! Do you feel like you're the boss of yourself? What have you unlocked about yourself?

You are your master. Only you have the
master keys to open the inner locks.

—Amit Ray

LOOKING BACK TO SEE FORWARD. Reflecting on the lessons you've learned on your journey helps prepare you for what's around the next bend.

WRITE NOW! When you look back on what you've seen on your journey so far, what do you think will come next?

PROGRESS, NOT PERFECTION. Reflect on your journal entries from the past week. Do you feel like you made progress? Do you feel like you enjoyed the journey and showed yourself love and care, or did you get hung up on perfection? Fill in the following progress bars to show how you feel about the week.

	1	5	10
Progress			
Enjoyment of the Journey			
Feelings of Self-Love			

WRITE NOW! What are your thoughts about this past week? Where did you make progress, and how did it feel?

THE CLOCK'S TICKING. Time is always moving forward and it's taking you with it. Like change, that's something you can be certain about. You can spend your time working toward your goal or you can spend it doing something else. You can even spend it working against your own best interests when you let things like fear or doubt convince you that your dream is too big or not worth it or is never going to happen. If you take a step back, you can see that each thing you do or don't do is a step toward or away from your goal. Even missteps bring you closer through their lessons.

WRITE NOW! How much time and energy are you regularly putting into working toward your goal? Can you make more time for it?

_____

_____

_____

_____

_____

_____

_____

If you don't make the time to work on creating the life you want, you're eventually going to be forced to spend a LOT of time dealing with a life you don't want.

—Kevin Ngo

IT HAPPENS! There's not a person out there who, in a dark hour, didn't feel like quitting. The successful ones are the people who kept going anyway.

WRITE NOW! Write a mantra to motivate you when you feel like quitting.

BEAT BACK BAD VIBES. There's not a person out there who doesn't feel just awful about themselves sometimes. The trick is reminding yourself of the truth when you feel that way.

WRITE NOW! Write a mantra to remind yourself of how flippin' awesome you truly are.

FEAR OF THE FINISH LINE. A strange quirk of human nature is that sometimes, when you're getting close to the end of a long journey, you can become afraid to finish it. When this happens, it's a subtle thing. You don't think, *Oh no, I don't want to finish this!* Instead, you start holding yourself back. You slack off when you don't need to, or you start obsessing about getting things perfect. At the heart of this fear can be any number of things, but most likely the journey has become a safe space and finishing means moving on to what's next. And change is scary.

WRITE NOW! Do you feel like you're at all afraid to finish your journey, or are you anxious as heck to reach your goal? Or both!?

HARD HAPPY. No matter what goal you've been working toward this whole time or the path you've chosen to take you to it, at heart these things should make you happy. Not the simple, easy happy that comes from watching your favorite TV show or savoring a good meal, but the real happy that is not easy to come by. The one that comes from hard work done with a purpose. The one that comes from resolve and overcoming obstacles. These are the things that make you feel great about yourself and, in turn, make you happy.

WRITE NOW! What about your journey has made you deeply happy?

The purpose of our life is to live a happy life.

—Tenzin Gyatso, the 14th Dalai Lama

DIG DEEP. It's easy to complain about how bad something is, but finding the positive in it will help you move forward, instead of keeping you stuck in the trap of indignation.

WRITE NOW! What's one crappy thing going on in your life and what good can you find in it?

_____

_____

_____

_____

PROGRESS, NOT PERFECTION. Reflect on your journal entries from the past week. Do you feel like you made progress? Do you feel like you enjoyed the journey and showed yourself love and care, or did you get hung up on perfection? Fill in the following progress bars to show how you feel about the week.

	1	5	10
Progress			
Enjoyment of the Journey			
Feelings of Self-Love			

WRITE NOW! What are your thoughts about this past week? Where did you make progress, and how did it feel?

_____

_____

FUN COMES WITH IT. This is it! The final month of your journal journey toward your goal. If you put in all this time and work, it's probably because you love what you're doing as well as where you're going. After all, the joy we get from the journey is what motivates us to do the work. What's more, just because something is hard doesn't mean it's not fun. In fact, when something is really hard and you totally nail it, that's the most fun you can have. It's exhilarating to feel you're at your best. What could be more fun than that?

WRITE NOW! Looking back over your journey, what was the most fun you had?

Having fun is not a diversion from a successful life; it is the pathway to it.

—Martha Beck

BUMPS IN THE ROAD. You visit many places along a journey, and not all of them feel great at the time. But they all teach you something.

WRITE NOW! Looking back, what was the low point of your journey and what did you learn from it?

INTO THE LIGHT. When you break through to the next level, the feeling you get is like no other.

WRITE NOW! What was your biggest breakthrough on your journey so far and how did it make you feel?

THIS MEANS SOMETHING. Going after your dream is one of the most meaningful things you can decide to do in your lifetime, and you're doing it! You set a goal and you're seeing it through. The experiences you have along the way—the lessons, the wins, the changes in how you feel about yourself and your role in the world—enrich you in ways that go well beyond your goal alone. They make you a purposeful person who knows their own tremendous worth. They make for a life well-lived.

WRITE NOW! What has been the most meaningful thing to you about your journey?

PROGRESS IS CHANGE. You wouldn't be working this hard if you didn't want something in your life to change. No matter what your goal is, you've had to make changes to get to it. Maybe you changed your priorities, the way you spend your time, the way you think about yourself, the things you believe you're capable of. This journey has been one of progress and progress is change, by definition. It's movement and transformation.

WRITE NOW! What's the biggest change you've seen over the past year?

_____   _____

_____

_____

_____

_____

_____

_____

_____

Dreams are lovely. But they are just dreams. Fleeting, ephemeral, pretty. But dreams do not come true just because you dream them. It's hard work that makes things happen. It's hard work that creates change.

—Shonda Rhimes

MORE TO COME. You've come so far and experienced so much, but there's still more road ahead of you, which means you still have a great deal to look forward to. Even when you've reached the goal you set for yourself, that success will have a resounding effect on your life.

WRITE NOW! What moment are you most looking forward to?

PROGRESS, NOT PERFECTION. Reflect on your journal entries from the past week. Do you feel like you made progress? Do you feel like you enjoyed the journey and showed yourself love and care, or did you get hung up on perfection? Fill in the following progress bars to show how you feel about the week.

	1	5	10
Progress			
Enjoyment of the Journey			
Feelings of Self-Love			

WRITE NOW! What are your thoughts about this past week? Where did you make progress, and how did it feel?

REAL VALUE. You deserve to be so proud of yourself. Instead of going on with your life doing what was easy and comfortable, you decided to do something of real value. You have chosen a path for yourself that requires hard work and dedication. And it's that effort that makes your goal so worthwhile. The payment you've made for it is your time, sweat, and tears, which are the dearest things you can give.

WRITE NOW! How do you value your journey and your goal?

_____   _____

_____

_____

_____

_____

_____

_____

_____

_____

What we obtain too cheap, we esteem too lightly: it is dearness only that gives everything its value.

—Thomas Paine

LET IT GO. When you started this journey you probably had some ideas about what would happen or what was important that you realize now don't serve you.

WRITE NOW! What did you start your journey with that you can now let go of?

_____

_____

_____

_____

_____

BRING IT IN. As you wound your way on your path, more than likely you have picked up some things that you didn't anticipate needing or wanting at the start of your journey.

WRITE NOW! What unexpected lessons or qualities have you picked up along your way?

_____

_____

_____

_____

_____

SINCE DAY 1. This journey has taken you a long way. When you first stepped foot on the path, you probably had some fears about whether or not you could or would do all the work it would take to reach your goal, but you made a commitment that day, and you've done a marvelous job keeping it. The rewards have hopefully been myriad, expanding past your goal alone and infusing you with strength and courage and abilities that are now so much a part of you that you carry them with you everywhere you go.

WRITE NOW! How are you different today than you were on the day you set out on your journey?

NOT WHAT YOU EXPECTED. As with any plan and grand journey, the plan and the reality of the trip are very different things. Things could look and feel different than you may have expected, and you're surprised by unexpected twists and turns. You might hate things you thought you would love and love things you thought you would hate. You might be going along and suddenly find yourself somewhere entirely different but even better than where you had originally planned to go. Being open to chance developments or unforeseen opportunities is part of what can take you to greater places than you even dreamed.

WRITE NOW! What has surprised you most along your journey?

_____

_____

_____

_____

_____

_____

_____

*Life is full of surprises and serendipity.
Being open to unexpected turns in the
road is an important part of success.*

—Condoleezza Rice

BETTER TODAY. There are surely loads of things you've improved at or learned to do over the past year, but perhaps there's one thing that stands out.

WRITE NOW! What can you do today that you couldn't do on Day 1 of your journey?

_____   _____

_____

_____

_____

_____

PROGRESS, NOT PERFECTION. Reflect on your journal entries from the past week. Do you feel like you made progress? Do you feel like you enjoyed the journey and showed yourself love and care, or did you get hung up on perfection? Fill in the following progress bars to show how you feel about the week.

	1	5	10
Progress			
Enjoyment of the Journey			
Feelings of Self-Love			

WRITE NOW! What are your thoughts about this past week? Where did you make progress, and how did it feel?

_____

_____

YOU DAY. Every day that you feel good about what you're doing, that you're proud of yourself and confident that you're nearing your goal is a day that you celebrate yourself. But after a year on the road, it's good to take some time to stop and wholeheartedly revel in your achievements. You deserve to take the time to recognize how far you've come and everything you've done along the way. You've done so much, and taking time to honor that is important.

WRITE NOW! How proud are you of yourself?

You have to celebrate every step you take in life. You have to see that there are possibilities for you to break through, even in the smallest steps.

—Olly Sanya

HAPPY ANNIVERSARY! Mark your one-year progress anniversary with something special, just for you.

WRITE NOW! How will you reward yourself for a yearlong job well done?

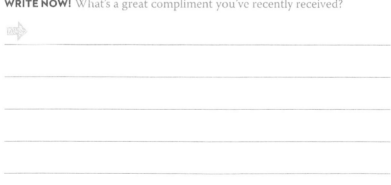

IT SHOWS. Other people have probably noticed and been impressed by your transformation over the past year.

WRITE NOW! What's a great compliment you've recently received?

ENJOYING THE JOURNEY? One massive key to achieving your goal is enjoying the journey getting there. This idea is something you've seen over and over again in this journal because it's vitally important. It's the metric you use to know if what you're doing is right, to tell if you're on the right path. If you find no joy or love in what you're doing, you have to ask yourself if the goal you're working toward is worth it—if it's really the goal for you. The joy you find on your journey is as important as the progress you make, so asking yourself if you're enjoying what you're doing is one of the most crucial questions you can ask.

WRITE NOW! How have you been enjoying your journey over the past year?

PATIENCE IS A VIRTUE. At this point, you might be really close to achieving your goal or you might still have a long road ahead of you. Depending on what you want to do, you might never be done. And even if you are just about done with this goal, there's always more journey ahead of you in life. Being patient, then, with yourself and the process makes the journey manageable, enjoyable. Without patience you will never feel like you're doing enough or that you're good enough. Without patience you give up or you burn out. But if you can be patient with yourself and happy with your progress one day at a time, you'll be continually rewarded for it.

WRITE NOW! Have you been patient with yourself?

_____

_____

_____

_____

_____

_____

_____

_____

Be patient with yourself.
Self-growth is tender; it's holy ground.
There's no greater investment.

—Stephen Covey

PAT YOURSELF ON THE BACK. Continue to celebrate yourself this week by taking some time to think about your most amazing qualities. Don't be shy about acknowledging and reveling in how great you are.

WRITE NOW! List five amazing things about yourself.

PROGRESS, NOT PERFECTION. Reflect on your journal entries from the past week. Do you feel like you made progress? Do you feel like you enjoyed the journey and showed yourself love and care, or did you get hung up on perfection? Fill in the following progress bars to show how you feel about the week.

	1	5	10
Progress			
Enjoyment of the Journey			
Feelings of Self-Love			

WRITE NOW! What are your thoughts about this past week? Where did you make progress, and how did it feel?

THE REAL GOAL. Who you've become over the past year is someone so dedicated, so capable, and so strong that you can do anything you set your mind to. While you were aiming at one goal all this time, you've achieved so much more than that in the pursuit. Regardless of what your goal is or was, through the purpose you felt in the journey, the confidence you built, and the capabilities you fostered, you have transformed yourself into the best *you* you can be, and that's what lies at the heart of any goal.

WRITE NOW! Who have you become on your journey?

_What you get by reaching your goals
is not nearly so important as what
you become by reaching them._

—Zig Ziglar

MAKING CHOICES. You had to make a lot of decisions over the past year about where to go, when, and how.

WRITE NOW! What's the best decision you made over the past year?

WISH IN ONE HAND. While missteps and mistakes are just lessons, sometimes there are things you wish you'd done differently. Thinking about what you wish you did instead can also teach you a lesson.

WRITE NOW! If you had it to do again, what, if anything, would you change about the past year?

TAKE A MOMENT. Practicing gratitude every day can help you be a happier person, but when you achieve something really big, it's that much more important to stop and take time to be grateful. Grateful for the goal you've reached, grateful to yourself for all the work you put in, grateful to others for their help, and grateful for life itself. Doing so honors the achievement and helps you savor the moment. It allows you a moment to be absolutely mindful of your success. You've come all this way, so give yourself some time to appreciate it.

WRITE NOW! What are you most grateful for from your journey?

YOU ARE THE JOURNEY. As long as you're alive, you're on a journey. You may have reached your goal over this past year, or you may still be working toward it. Either way, it's the progress that counts. It's the journey that matters. And that journey hasn't ended just because you've reached the last week in this journal. You are still on a path and you can decide where it takes you. You can choose to keep getting better, to keep growing, to keep getting stronger and kinder and more loving. The journey is yours and you are what you make of it.

WRITE NOW! What's next for you?

For me, becoming isn't about arriving somewhere or achieving a certain aim. I see it instead as forward motion, a means of evolving, a way to reach continuously toward a better self. The journey doesn't end.

—Michelle Obama

ALL ROADS ARE OPEN. There is a big, wide world out there, and you can go anywhere you want.

WRITE NOW! What are you most looking forward to?

_____

_____

_____

_____

_____

PROGRESS, NOT PERFECTION. Reflect on your journal entries from the past week. Do you feel like you made progress? Do you feel like you enjoyed the journey and showed yourself love and care, or did you get hung up on perfection? Fill in the following progress bars to show how you feel about the week.

	1	5	10
Progress			
Enjoyment of the Journey			
Feelings of Self-Love			

WRITE NOW! What are your thoughts about this past week? Where did you make progress, and how did it feel?

_____

_____

Contributor's List

MAYA ANGELOU—American author

MINNA THOMAS ANTRIM—Early twentieth-century American writer

LUCILLE BALL—American actor and studio executive

MARTHA BECK—American life coach

ROY T. BENNETT—American inspirational author

BERNARD BERKOWITZ—American professor

HARRIET BRAIKER—American psychologist and author

PAM BROWN—American inspirational author

BUDDHA—Ancient Indian founder of Buddhism

VALORIE BURTON—American life coach

OCTAVIA BUTLER—American science fiction author

JULIA CAMERON—American artist and author

SHERRIE CAMPBELL—American psychologist

PEMA CHÖDRÖN—American Buddhist leader and author

WINSTON CHURCHILL—British prime minister (1940–45; 1951–55)

JAMES CLEAR—American inspirational author

NICKY CLINCH—American holistic counselor

ALAN COHEN—American inspirational author

ROBERT COLLIER—American self-help author

STEPHEN COVEY—American educator

MIHALY CSIKSZENTMIHALYI—Hungarian-American psychologist

ROWENA CORY DANIELLS—Australian fantasy author

GLENNON DOYLE—American self-help author

KATHERINE DUNN—American horror author

WILL DURANT—American historian

WAYNE W. DYER—American self-help author

DEBRA ECKERLING—American goal coach

RALPH WALDO EMERSON—Nineteenth-century American essayist and philosopher

MASARU EMOTO—Japanese spirituality author

DOUGLAS H. EVERETT—English chemist

SALLY FIELD—American actor

JANE FONDA—American actor

MARGOT FONTEYN—English ballerina

MARIE FORLEO—American entrepreneur

ALISSON FURMAN—American businesswoman

DIANE VON FURSTENBERG—Belgian fashion designer

GAIL LYNNE GOODWIN—American entrepreneur

TENZIN GYATSO—His Holiness the 14th Dalai Lama

MANDY HALE—American inspirational author

NOELLE HANCOCK—American reporter

LOUISE HAY—American self-help author

LEWIS HOWES—American athlete

JANIS IAN—American singer-songwriter

KYLE JESSEN—American self-help writer

ERICA JONG—American feminist author

MICHAEL JORDAN—American athlete

RACHEL KANG—American inspirational speaker

SUZY KASSEM—Egyptian American writer

HELEN KELLER—American disability rights advocate

SØREN KIERKEGAARD—Nineteenth-century Danish philosopher

CHANDA KOCHHAR—Indian businesswoman

MARIE KONDO—Japanese organizing expert

SARAH LEWIS—American history professor

SOPHIA LOREN—Italian actor

MEGHAN MARKLE—Duchess of Sussex and actor

RALPH MARSTON—American athlete

ABRAHAM MASLOW—American psychologist

THOMAS MERTON—American Trappist monk and writer

TESS MILLER—American psychologist

ELON MUSK—South African-born businessman

MILDRED NEWMAN—Twentieth-century American psychologist

KEVIN NGO—American motivational author

BARBARA OAKLEY—American engineer and education writer

MICHELLE OBAMA—First Lady of the US (2009–17), American attorney and writer

SAM OWEN—American psychologist and writer

THOMAS PAINE—Eighteenth-century English American philosopher

BOB PARSONS—American entrepreneur

MEERA LEE PATEL—American artist and self-help author

AMY POEHLER—American comedian and actor

POLYBIUS—Ancient Greek historian

JESSIE POTTER—Twentieth-century educator

AMIT RAY—Indian spiritual writer

SHONDA RHIMES—American television producer

CONDOLEEZZA RICE—American diplomat and former secretary of state

RAINER MARIA RILKE—Early twentieth-century Austrian poet and novelist

THEODORE ROOSEVELT—US president (1901–9)

ELEANOR ROOSEVELT—First Lady of the US (1933–45), diplomat, and activist

KAREN SALMANSOHN—American self-help author

OLLY SANYA—American motivational speaker

ROBERT H. SCHULLER—Christian televangelist

WILLIAM SHAKESPEARE—Sixteenth-century English playwright

W. L. SHELDON—Twentieth-century American ethicist

JEN SINCERO—American motivational writer

SIMON SINEK—English American inspirational writer

PIERS STEEL—American researcher

JOHN STEINBECK—American author

GLORIA STEINEM—American feminist journalist

ELLEN SUE STERN—American self-help author

ROBERT LOUIS STEVENSON—Nineteenth-century Scottish novelist and writer

MURIEL STRODE—Early twentieth-century American poet

BEN SWEET—Unknown

JAIME TARDY—American business coach

DWAYNE THOMAS—American inspirational writer

VIRGIL—Ancient Roman poet

BOOKER T. WASHINGTON—Nineteenth-century American educator, author, and presidential advisor

GERARD WAY—American singer and comic book writer

SQUIRE BILL WIDENER—Late nineteenth-century American teacher

MARIANNE WILLIAMSON—American self-help writer

SUSAN B. WILSON—American leadership coach

OPRAH WINFREY—American media magnate and actor

JEANETTE WINTERSON—English writer

ZIG ZIGLAR—American motivational author

Notes

Notes

Notes

Notes

Notes

Notes